MW01136556

# GREAT

DISCOVER THE GREAT PLAINS

*Series Editor:* Richard Edwards

RICHARD EDWARDS

# PLAINS

# Homesteaders

UNIVERSITY OF NEBRASKA PRESS *Lincoln*

The University of Nebraska Press is part of a land-
grant institution with campuses and programs
on the past, present, and future homelands of
the Pawnee, Ponca, Otoe-Missouria, Omaha,
Dakota, Lakota, Kaw, Cheyenne, and Arapaho
Peoples, as well as those of the relocated Ho-
Chunk, Sac and Fox, and Iowa Peoples.

Library of Congress Cataloging-
in-Publication Data
Names: Edwards, Richard, 1944– author.
Title: Great Plains homesteaders
/ Richard Edwards.
Description: Lincoln: University of Nebraska
Press, [2024] | Series: Discover the Great Plains
| Includes bibliographical references and index.
Identifiers: LCCN 2024009775
ISBN 9781496238948 (paperback)
ISBN 9781496240590 (epub)
ISBN 9781496240606 (pdf)
Subjects: LCSH: Frontier and pioneer life—Great
Plains. | African American pioneers—Great
Plains—History. | Frontier and pioneer life—
Great Plains. | Great Plains—History. | BISAC:
HISTORY / United States / State & Local /
Midwest (IA, IL, IN, KS, MI, MN, MO, ND,
NE, OH, SD, WI) | HISTORY / United States /
State & Local / Southwest (AZ, NM, OK, TX)
Classification: LCC F596 .E39 2024 |
DDC 978—dc23/eng/20240229
LC record available at
https://lccn.loc.gov/2024009775

Set in Garamond Premier Pro by Lacey Losh.
Designed by N. Putens.

*The days of the pioneers are passing. Only a few, like the last leaves upon a cottonwood in November, linger to whisper the tales of industry's conquest of the romantic west. Perhaps before the Great Spirit has called all these golden leaves home, a Longfellow, a Whittier, or a Lowell shall arise, and with Homeric pen, translate to the written page the epic and the drama of the plains.*

—*Custer County* (Nebraska) *Chief* on the death of an eighty-one-year-old homesteader, December 16, 1930

# CONTENTS

# ILLUSTRATIONS

**Fig. 1.** Map of the Great Plains. Courtesy of the Center for Great Plains Studies.

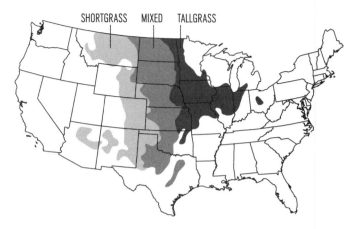

**Fig. 2.** Map of tallgrass, mixed-grass, and shortgrass prairies prior to European settlement. Map by Katie Nieland.

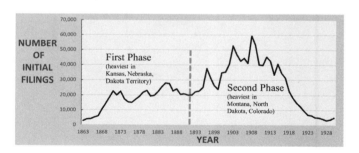

**Fig. 3.** Graph of two phases of homesteading claims in the United States (thirty homesteading states). Initial filings that were later successfully proved up, by year. Based on U.S. Department of the Interior, *Homesteads* (Washington DC: Bureau of Land Management, 1962).

GREAT PLAINS HOMESTEADERS

# CHAPTER ONE

# Homesteaders

They were a phenomenon. Nearly three million of them tried to take up the government's dare—"bet you a quarter section you can't last five years on our prairie land"—and 1.6 million succeeded. Including family members, ten million or more people moved west to try their luck. Their numbers paralleled those of the Great Migration of Black people out of the South to northern cities. The homesteaders claimed 285 million acres, amounting to 15 percent of the land area of the Lower 48 states. The majority, 960,000, settled in the Great Plains, where they gained patents (title) to 180 million acres of prairie. That was nearly as much land as in the thirteen original American colonies. Most homesteaders became owners of 160 acres, but some got less and some more.

They came from all over. Most were whites, but they included Black people, too. Both men and women filed claims. They came from all regions of the United States: from both British and French Canada, Norway, Germany, Britain, Sweden, Russia, Switzerland, Austria, Denmark, France, Italy, and even Arab lands. They represented thirty or forty nationalities and many languages. They brought all varieties of Christianity. They included Jews and Muslims as well.

They came because the government offered them a quarter section (160 acres) of "free land." True, you had to work for it.

After filing and paying a small fee, the homesteader had to build a dwelling, live on the claim for five years, and cultivate at least ten acres. (The government slightly revised these requirements over the years). At "proving up," they provided affidavits and other documents to show the General Land Office (GLO) that they had met all the law's requirements. Some months later, the GLO mailed them their patents. For millions who feared they would never be able to own land, it was a godsend.

The Homestead Act of 1862 directed land offices to begin accepting claims on January 1, 1863. Few land seekers filed claims until the Civil War ended in 1865, but by 1868 they started showing up in large numbers.

Most came to the Great Plains, an enormous grassland stretching west. Gateway cities—Kansas City, Omaha, Sioux Falls, Fargo—ringed its eastern border. On its west edge, Billings, Cheyenne, and the growing metropolis of Denver marked where the prairie gave way to the Rockies' foothills. The grassland ranged from Oklahoma to the Canadian border (and beyond, but we do not consider Canada here). In its vast spaces there were virtually no cities. The Great Plains offered 350 million acres of unbroken prairie.

The homesteaders' migration crested in two great waves. The first phase lasted from 1868 to the mid-1890s. Homesteaders journeyed in their prairie schooners and wagons to fill up the central plains of Kansas, Nebraska, and eastern Dakota Territory. These areas accounted for 38 percent of all claims, leaving the remainder scattered among the other twenty-five homesteading states. Large numbers continued arriving until about 1892, when hard times for farmers and a deep national depression discouraged further migration.

Better times returned later in the 1890s, stimulating homesteading's second phase. With the central plains mostly filled up, new migrants were forced to file their claims in more peripheral areas. They rode the railway spur lines to the end of newly laid tracks. Then they took to wagons, or even Model Ts, to penetrate the remote, marginal reaches of the plains. Claimants focused on North Dakota, Colorado, and Montana. This phase lasted until the early 1920s.

The agricultural depression of the 1920s and the Great Depression of the 1930s ended homesteading. Congress repealed the homesteading law in 1976, except for in Alaska. The last homesteaders filed claims in Alaska in the 1980s.

The government wanted these homesteaders to succeed. National leaders saw "unimproved" prairie as simply unproductive land. But officials set the homesteaders a horrendously difficult task in asking them to turn the harsh prairie environment into productive farms. Some claimants arrived with farming experience; others came fresh from factories or city occupations unadorned with agrarian skills. But few were ready to farm in the semi-arid, windblown Great Plains.

Many initial filers failed, perhaps as many as 45 percent. They were inept farmers or suffered bad luck or bad timing or got injured. Some fell deep into debt and couldn't get out. Some couldn't stand the blistering summers and frigid winters. Others suffered loneliness, anxiety, or a pervasive sense of failure and hopelessness, and so they gave up. The causes of failure were myriad.

Some failed because they were so poor. Most homesteaders arrived with few possessions, and they were chronically short of cash. So to get started, many had to borrow. Thor and Gjertru Birkelo left Norway in 1904 to homestead in the Big Meadow township of Williams County, North Dakota. They borrowed money to migrate, so they were already in debt when they arrived. After filing, Thor borrowed money from his brother Kristen to buy two horses, a wagon, a plow, and harnesses—essential equipment for getting his farm going. In

1905 he borrowed from Kristen to buy a cow, in 1906 another cow, in 1907 a second team of horses.

In 1908 a finance company gave the Birkelos a $600 mortgage on condition that they use $200 to commute (buy) their claim. Now, as owners, they could legally offer their farm as loan collateral. But even with these infusions of cash, the Birkelos kept falling deeper into debt. In 1919 they borrowed $4,506 to consolidate their debts, but they could not make the payments. In 1924 the investment company holding their mortgage foreclosed, and the Birkelos lost their farm. They had gone from landless in Norway to landless in America in twenty hard years.

Some people thought that if the government was going to give them a nice 160-acre farm, why, they'd take it! All you had to do was live on it for five years and make some small improvements, and who couldn't do that? Owning land seemed as desirable in the nineteenth century as owning Apple stock is in the twenty-first.

Solomon Butcher was one who tried. He filed a homestead claim in 1888 in eastern Custer County, Nebraska. But he quit after only two weeks. It was too hot, too dirty, and too buggy for him. "Any man that would leave the luxuries of a boarding house, where they had hash every day, to [turn] Nebraska sod . . . was a fool," he said. He switched to photography. And it was fortunate for us that he did—he bequeathed to us the best collection of nineteenth-century homesteader photographs we have. Others like Butcher, of the educated and more affluent classes, had easier options than homesteading available to them, and few of them filed claims.

While many claimants failed, more succeeded than failed. Roughly 55 percent of initial filers earned their patents. They succeeded through some combination of smarter choices, harder work, more self-denial, and better luck. They avoided debilitating injury and illness. They dodged hail damage and grasshoppers. Whatever their successful formula, they brought grit and determination to transform the land and create new lives out of the opportunity that homesteading gave them.

They overcame many perils. No need for Hollywood writers of the long-running TV show *Little House on the Prairie* to dream up fake misfortunes and phony courage. Take for example the homesteaders who settled on the banks of Victoria Creek in Custer County, Nebraska. During the spring and early summer of 1879, they saw their crops growing bountifully. The buoyant community gathered on the Fourth of July to celebrate the holiday.

They noticed a small, dark cloud emerge in the northwest. Then, with great suddenness, it spread across the whole sky. The heavens unleashed a violent hailstorm. Celebrants scurried into the small log schoolhouse for safety, some crying, many praying. The hail broke all the school's windows. When the storm had passed, the families hurried to their farms to inspect the damage. They found their crops completely destroyed. The hail had beaten the plants right into the ground. The settlers harvested no grain that year.

Homesteaders faced killing cold and blinding blizzards. In 1909 Elizabeth Corey homesteaded in Stanley County in central South Dakota. She lived in her flimsy shack while she taught school. It was already so cold in November that, when she woke up, she found the water in her pail frozen solid. By December she found "everything froze up tight as a brick . . . apples, potatoes, and all rattle around like stones." Even walking home from the neighbors' was dangerous, and they tried to persuade her that she should sleep at their house on the coldest nights, fearing she would freeze to death in her own place. But she was hardy. When she woke up in the morning, she had "got used to having my hair, eyebrows and eyewinkers covered with frost and ice."

On the warm, springlike morning of January 12, 1888, Nebraska homesteader Aaron Lenstrom left his Custer County homestead. He was traveling to the North Loup valley to help his neighbor haul some hay. Just when he reached the hayfield, the weather turned, and a howling blizzard struck. The storm engulfed all of Nebraska, stopping Burlington & Rock Island trains right on the tracks. Randolph Hanna was in a saloon in Falls City in far southeast Nebraska when the storm struck. He got drunk and then tried to walk the three miles back to his homestead. His hands became so frostbitten a doctor had to amputate them.

Three hundred miles to the northwest, outside O'Neill, Nebraska, two girls, aged thirteen and eight, tried to walk home from school but didn't make it, freezing to death just a mile from safety. An estimated 235 people, many of them schoolchildren, died, giving the storm its name: the Children's Blizzard of 1888.

Aaron Lenstrom, returning from the hayfield in the North Loup valley, was lucky. He tied himself to his wagon and let his team of mules use their natural instincts to find their way home. They crossed several fences, and where the fence ran down to the river, the mules walked out on the ice to get around them. To the great relief of his family waiting in their dugout, Lenstrom arrived home safely.

Anders Svendsbye, a Norwegian immigrant, homesteaded in Williams County in northwest North Dakota in 1904. The region suffered winter storms so powerful that snow drifts sometimes completely covered the houses. After one storm, Svendsbye had to break a window and dig up through the snow to free his family. He broke a hole in the barn roof to lower a bucket to water the animals.

Another time Svendsbye was returning from the nearby town of Tioga with a team and wagon when he ran into a sudden violent blizzard. The snow blowing into his face blinded him so completely he couldn't see the road at all. He decided to trust his team to find the way back to his homestead. He tied the reins to the wagon box and turned his back to the storm. A few hours later the horses pulled up short, their noses touching the corner of Svendsbye's house.

Homesteaders farmed far from medical care, so they doctored themselves. Adaline Hagey homesteaded by herself near relatives in Mountrail County, North Dakota, in the early 1900s. As recounted by family members, one day when she was chopping firewood, the axe slipped in her hand, and she sliced a deep cut in her arm. No matter: she retrieved her sewing kit from her sod house and sewed up her arm herself. She then finished chopping her wood. Adaline was my great-grandmother.

Many homesteaders, successful ones as well as those who failed, faced loneliness, depression, despair. Thomas Raaen migrated from Norway after being kicked out of the Norwegian army for excessive drinking. In Iowa he got sober. He met and married Ragnhild Redningen. In 1874 Thomas filed a homestead claim in Steele County in eastern Dakota Territory. Though he proved up successfully, he and Ragnhild had a hard time making their farm pay.

Under the stress of failure and poverty Thomas started drinking again. His daughter claimed he was a moral man of scrupulous honesty when sober, but he was a mean drunk. He squandered the family's meager wheat income on alcohol, making their survival depend on Ragnhild's egg and butter sales. Thomas, in his drunken furies, beat Ragnhild. One time when she hid his booze, he became so enraged he knocked several of her teeth out. They stayed on the farm for thirty years.

Homesteaders faced other kinds of dangers, too. Edgar and Josephine Denio moved to their homestead in Custer County, Nebraska, in July 1874. Edgar dug a cellar and collected building materials to construct a house. He prepared four acres for planting. But then Edgar either had an accident or got sick, and they ran out of money—in any event, he could not build the house himself, and they lacked money to hire someone to build it for them. In 1876 Edgar died, leaving Josephine to homestead alone. Following General Land Office (GLO) rules, Edgar had filed the homestead in his own name as "head of household." The GLO was only beginning to implement procedures for widows to take over their dead husbands' claims. Eight months later Josephine was finally able to prove up, but by then she was left to farm by herself, which had never been her plan.

One who had the grit and determination to succeed was Jenny Fletcher. She had come out with her husband Z.T. to homestead at the Nicodemus colony in Graham County, Kansas. The colonists had a very rough first year. Few had savings, but even those with money had to travel thirty-seven miles to Ellis over prairie trails to find shops carrying the shovels and winter coats and flour they needed. "That was the darkest period that I have experienced since I crossed the Mississippi," Jenny recalled.

Z.T. had gone to Topeka to work, and he sent Jenny some money. But she had no place to spend it when the weather turned cold and snow drifts blocked the trails. No traders showed up wanting to sell supplies. The settlers went without bread for more than a month. Finally, a man with some rye to sell passed through. "We boiled the rye and ate it without seasoning, not even salting it, as we had no salt," she recalled. Jenny and Z.T. stuck it out and made a home for themselves on the prairie.

The homesteaders also lived at the mercy of eastern power brokers—the railroads, big grain millers, finance companies, and banks. Railroad companies maintained extortionate freight rates that reduced the price farmers received for their crops and raised the cost of farm machinery and other items they purchased. Farmers suffered when the national economy broke down, as it did in the 1870s, the 1890s, and the 1930s. These were just more troubles, like the blizzards and hail and grasshoppers, that lay beyond the homesteaders' control.

Despite the obstacles and setbacks, many homesteaders persisted to achieve their dreams. Will Trew and wife Ella homesteaded in Custer County, Nebraska, in 1880. Will was born and educated in Ohio; Ella, in Massachusetts. Will arrived in Nebraska first, in 1871, as a member of the Soldiers Free Homestead Colony in the tiny settlement of Gibbon in Buffalo County. He soon moved to Custer County, where he and Ella took up a homestead along the South Loup River. He built a sixteen-by-twenty-four-foot log house with three rooms. It had a dirt floor and sod roof.

There the Trews raised five children and worked patiently to build their farm. They grew corn and other row crops, and they raised cattle and hogs, which they shipped to market. During the half-century they spent on the homestead, they expanded their holdings, eventually owning 1,400 acres. Will became president of a small bank in Sumner, Nebraska.

In 1930, when Will was eighty-one, he went out to check on a pasture cistern he believed was leaking. Some hours later, when he failed to return, his grandson and others went looking for him. They found Will's car parked by the cistern. They searched the cistern's murky water and found Will's body lying at the bottom. The men surmised he had lost his balance or his ladder broke, and he hit his head as he fell in. A tall man, he probably could have stood up in the cistern's five feet of water if he hadn't been stunned, but instead he drowned. Ella died in 1938. Their sons, George, Leon, and Nelson, continued the farming operation, and after them, Will and Ella's grandchildren farmed the land, too.

Like the Trews, many other homesteaders prospered. Gudrun and Anders Svendsbye created a multigenerational wheat farm

**Fig. 4.** Gudrun and Anders Svendsbye on their homestead in Williams County, North Dakota, circa 1915. Courtesy of the Vatne family.

in Williams County, North Dakota. In the photograph, they stand in a farm wagon, sturdy settlers building their new life. Decades later their grandson, Kenneth Vatne, farmed the land as his own. Among others we will meet later, Henry and Rosie Ise built a prosperous, long-surviving family farm and became valued members of their community in Osborne County, Kansas. Henry and Mary Burden raised eight children on their productive Saline County, Nebraska, homestead. The Trews, Svensdbyes, Ises, and Burdens and nearly a million other homesteading families overcame the Great Plains' severe challenges to survive and thrive.

Fashionable East Coast society, whom today we might call "influencers," scorned and mocked them as unsophisticated rubes. The smart set rendered one of the region's greatest champions, William Jennings Bryan, into a pathetic joke, despite his charismatic populist campaigns on behalf of poor and oppressed farmers and workers.

Like their homesteading ancestors, descendants who stayed in the region live in a culturally scorned region now dismissed as "flyover country." In one *Law and Order* episode the FBI hid a Mafia hit man in Las Vegas in its witness protection program. When he is unmasked, they offer him a chance to go back into hiding in Omaha, but he rejects it. "Omaha? Who goes to Omaha?" he mocks. Millions, it turns out. They passed through Omaha and other gateway cities to reach the beckoning lands beyond.

In what follows, I tell the homesteaders' story as much as possible through their own experiences. The histories come from homestead records, diaries, letters, news stories, county memorials, accounts by travelers and witnesses, ancestry records, official documents, and other sources. I focus only on the *homesteading phase* of settlement, not the subsequent fate of Great Plains agriculture, with its cycles of prosperity and hardship.

When I refer to *homesteaders* I mean to include all the participants—wives, husbands, children, and other relatives and members living in the household. The Homestead Act named only the head of household, a man unless no man was present, as "the" homesteader, and the GLO also followed this practice. But all members of the household experienced the hardships and joys of homesteading, and all contributed to the family's success or failure.

"To this day, the Homestead Act remains the most comprehensive form of wealth redistribution that has ever taken place in America," observed historian Kari Leigh Merritt in 2017. It benefited "both native poor whites and white immigrants," she said. (It also benefited smaller numbers of Black people.) "Homesteading offered them a chance to start fresh. . . . Indeed, the importance of the Homestead Act cannot be overstated." She was correct about the importance of the Act but not quite accurate about what caused the redistribution.

The law itself transferred no land—it only enabled homesteaders to trigger a transfer. Only their grit and toil, their five years' residence in dugouts and sod houses and tarpaper shacks, their daring and determination and dreams, won them ownership of the land. That so many so eagerly took up the government's challenge and stuck it out to earn their patents was indeed phenomenal.

They created a stable middle-class society of small property owners. They transformed the Great Plains, America's great central grassland, as well as eastern Oregon and Washington, into the critical food-producing regions we rely on today. And they left a lasting mark on American culture.

Every homesteader's experience was different, as particular and distinct as the individual homesteader himself or herself. Yet their collective story, with all its hardships and toil and ambitions and setbacks, its hopes and fresh starts, its failures and successes, is central to the American experience.

Jules Haumont recalled his fresh start when he homesteaded with his uncles in Custer County, Nebraska. He remembered their poverty: "We came here to this beautiful country, in those early days, young, strong, healthy, filled with hope, energy, ambition. Poor, it is true. I remember the time I did not have the money to buy a postage stamp." But he also recalled their soaring hopes: "Oh! how poor in worldly good, but rich beyond dreams, in everything that makes life worthwhile. I do not know how large a bank account some of the old settlers may have today. I do not care, they will never be as rich as I felt when I first settled on my homestead."

# CHAPTER TWO

# Origins of the Homesteading Idea

How did homesteading come about, anyway? Giving away free land is rare. It happened before, but not often. Julius Caesar granted farms to his demobilized legionnaires, as did the Continental Congress for George Washington's veterans, but in those cases land was payment for service. Catherine the Great and grandson Alexander I offered free land to German farmers if they would settle in Russia. But such cases are infrequent in history.

It was by no means certain that the U.S. Government would offer free farms to people willing to settle its western lands. For its first seven decades, the government sold land rather than gave it away. But in the years leading up to the Civil War, Americans engaged in a great debate: What should the United States do with all the land between Omaha and California? They would spill blood on the Civil War's killing fields to decide that question.

The United States acquired its immense western domain—the land lying west of the Missouri River and west of Louisiana—in huge chunks. In 1803 President Thomas Jefferson bought the Louisiana Purchase, including all the land from New Orleans and Oklahoma to Iowa, the Dakotas, and Montana. In 1845 the United States annexed Texas. In 1846 the United States ended its border dispute with Britain and gained sovereignty over the future states of Oregon, Washington, and Idaho. In

1848 Congress collected the spoils from the Mexican-American War and annexed a huge area in the Southwest from Colorado to California.

The newly acquired lands remained largely a mystery to most Americans. People knew most about the far coast, which Spanish, British, and American ships had long explored. California, site of the 1849 gold discoveries, became a state in 1850. Oregon, the destination for thousands of migrants heading up the Oregon Trail, became a state in 1859.

But the interior West remained largely unknown. Stephen H. Long led a scientific expedition through the region in 1820 and had (misleadingly) labeled the grassland as the "Great American Desert." The newly won Southwest was connected to the eastern states only by the perilous Santa Fe Trail, which carefully skirted the great Comanche empire. Most traffic got to California by crossing the Isthmus of Panama or risking the long journey around Cape Horn in order to avoid the even more difficult trip across the interior. For most Americans the endless grassland and forbidding mountains formed an unfortunate barrier to the good stuff, the valuable lands on the Pacific coast.

Americans nonetheless held strong and bitterly incompatible views about what should happen in the interior West. In the 1840s and 1850s the nation was divided into two increasingly hostile camps: slave and free. Each had its vision for the future of the West.

The southern slave-owning elite, sometimes called the Slave Power, wanted to make the West a new slave realm. Their economy concentrated on cotton and was built on the labor of four million Black slaves. Slaveowners had already made a first migration, from the exhausted soils of the tobacco regions around Chesapeake Bay to the fabulously rich river bottoms of the Deep South. We still use expressions, surviving from that time and meaning *disaster*, when we say that something "went south" or was "sold down the river."

Slaveowners worried that when they needed to move or expand again, Where would they find new land? They looked longingly at annexing Cuba and Nicaragua, but mostly they eyed the West. The West would not only provide them new plantation fields; it would also furnish new slave states (and senators) to offset the entry of new free states like Oregon and Maine. President Polk, a Southerner, had provoked the Mexican war, and southern leaders now wanted to make the land west of Omaha a new slave empire.

Opposing them, northern advocates of "free labor" were equally determined to prevent slavery from spreading into the West. The Republican Party arose in the 1850s by insisting that the West be reserved for small farmers, not plantations. A growing abolitionist movement in the North challenged the legitimacy of slavery.

Stephen A. Douglas, "The Little Giant," and his foot-taller opponent Abraham Lincoln debated slavery during the Illinois Senate campaign in 1858. Their seven debates captured the nation's attention. The argument turned on exactly this question: Would slavery, as Abraham Lincoln wanted, be prohibited in the West and limited to the states where it already existed? Or would, as Stephen Douglas demanded, the (white, male) inhabitants of each new state be able to decide for themselves whether to allow slavery or not?

Lincoln warned, "A house divided against itself cannot stand. . . . It will become all one thing, or all the other. Either the opponents of slavery will arrest the further spread of it . . . Or its advocates shall push it forward, till it shall become lawful alike in all the States, old as well as new."

And, Lincoln said, the Slave Power was already winning this fight. After all, slaveowners had won a major victory in

**Fig. 5.** Abraham Lincoln and Stephen A. Douglas debate on the spread of slavery, Illinois, 1858. From Francis F. Browne, *The Everyday Life of Abraham Lincoln* (Chicago: N. D. Thompson, 1886).

1850 when Congress passed the Fugitive Slave Act. It required Northern states to capture and return runaways. The Slave Power triumphed again in 1854 when Congress passed the Kansas-Nebraska Act. This law repealed the Missouri Compromise of 1820, which had restricted slavery to states below the Mason-Dixon Line. The new act granted voters of each new western state the power to decide for themselves whether to permit slavery or not.

Then, in 1857, the Supreme Court shut the door to challenges of the Slave Power's dominance. It issued its heavy-handed *Dred Scott* decision. The court declared that slaveowners maintained their "property" right in slaves, even when they took their slaves to free states. Moreover, the court declared, Americans of African descent could never be U.S. citizens and had no rights that whites were bound to respect.

As Lincoln saw it in 1858, the issue was not to be whether slavery would survive in the South but, much more ominously, whether the South would force the rest of the nation to adopt its perverse system. The West was the test case for America. And *homesteading was the antislavers' proposed solution.*

While leaders debated the principles, ordinary folks took action on the ground. Proslavery and abolitionist settlers poured into Kansas ahead of that state's vote. They raided each other's settlements and murdered families in a conflict that came to be known as "Bleeding Kansas." And poor whites, hungry for land, began entering the vast Nebraska Territory to squat or "pre-empt" land. Squatting was illegal, but government lacked the means (or maybe the desire) to hold the squatters back. Congress responded to squatting's reality by periodically passing new preemption laws, each more accommodating to the squatters' rights.

Republicans believed homesteading was the answer to this chaos and to the threat of slavery's expansion. They proposed that the government move away from selling its land in big tracts that only rich people could afford to buy. Instead it should give land to "actual settlers." They hoped to create a yeomanry of small landowners on the public domain, land going neither to slaveowners nor greedy speculators. Many groups had favored passage of a homestead law, including Northern Whigs, the Liberty Party, Free-Soilers, Northern Democrats disaffected by Southern Democrats' growing insistence that they support slavery, a few lonely Southern pro-homesteaders like Andrew Johnson, and "western" interests generally.

Southern congressmen and senators, with a few dissenters, hated the "free land" idea. During the 1840s and 1850s they blocked passage of several proposed homesteading bills. In early 1860 homesteading advocates finally succeeded in getting Congress to approve a homestead act, but President James Buchanan, a Pennsylvanian who sympathized with the South, vetoed it.

Republicans, in their 1860 platform, promised to leave slavery alone in the states where it already existed, but they insisted on banning it in the western territories. And they promised to pass a homestead act.

Democrats, meeting in Charleston, South Carolina, split their party on the issue. Southern Democrats insisted that the platform include an iron pledge that slavery would be permitted in the territories. Northern Democrats refused, knowing such a pledge would lose them many voters and seats in the North. The Southerners walked out. In separate conventions later, Southern Democrats and Northern Democrats each nominated their own candidate for president.

Lincoln won the presidential election in 1860, and Republicans won most congressional elections in the North and West. Proslavery Democrats swept congressional seats in the South and won some congressional elections elsewhere. Democrats elected enough members to the Senate to gridlock anything Lincoln proposed, including a homestead bill.

But the Slave Power interpreted Lincoln's election as a mortal attack on the South, and eleven slave states seceded to form the Confederate States of America. Southern and Northern armies mobilized for the titanic battles to come, starting with the Battle of Bull Run in July 1861. Nearly all Southern representatives withdrew from Congress, leaving the Republicans in overwhelming control of both houses of Congress as well as of the executive branch.

With the Southerners now absent, Congress easily passed the Homestead Act, and on May 20, 1862, President Lincoln signed it into law. Daniel Freeman, a Union veteran, filed the nation's first homestead claim on January 1, 1863, in Beatrice, Nebraska. The great debate over what to do with the West was over, and the homesteading vision had won.

The land the government was offering to homesteaders, however, was not empty. Lewis and Clark's two-year expedition explored the region from St. Louis to where the Columbia River empties into the Pacific. They returned in 1806 with their report extolling the West's enormous spaces, its grand rivers and majestic mountains, its vast diversity of plants and colossal herds of game—and its many tribes of Indigenous peoples. The government would spend the next few decades wresting the land from Indians.

The outcome of the struggle was never in doubt. The United States had thirty or fifty million people (depending on the year) and access to industrial weaponry. It confronted, in the Great Plains, one or two hundred thousand Natives, who relied on trade with whites to obtain their guns and ammunition. The largest assembly of Native troops was probably the several thousand warriors under Sitting Bull and Crazy Horse who fought Custer at Little Bighorn in 1876. But the Indians' numbers were miniscule compared to the more than two million soldiers the Union had mobilized just eleven years earlier to fight the Confederacy.

Despite this disparity, the federal dispossession of Indians was nonetheless marked by a thoroughly shameful record of false dealing. Commissioners, Indian agents, and U.S. Army officers used suspect treaties that nonliterate Native leaders could not read. They cynically distributed alcohol and other destabilizing trade goods. They operated with lies and deceit. They bribed Indian leaders. And they employed other dishonest and discreditable practices to pressure Indians to give up legal claims to their land.

Whites pressed in from all sides. They disrupted Native societies in many ways, both unintentional and unofficial as well as deliberate policy. Hundreds of thousands of migrants passed through the Great Plains on their way to the goldfields in California, farms in Oregon and Utah, and mining camps in Colorado and Nevada. Along the way, they killed the game or drove it away. Commercial hunters exterminated eight to ten million bison in little more than a decade, between 1871 and 1883. They took only the hides, for which there was a lucrative market to make machinery drive belts for eastern and European factories. The incursion of so many whites passing through along with the extirpation of the buffalo weakened Indian nations throughout the region.

Whites bound for the West Coast unintentionally spread diseases previously unknown among Natives, who had little or no immunity. In the winter of 1831–32, smallpox killed five to six thousand Pawnee along the Platte River, cutting that nation's population in half. In 1837 a great smallpox epidemic in North Dakota killed 90 percent of the Mandan.

Wars among tribal nations disrupted the tribes' annual buffalo hunts and placed additional stress on them. The expansion of the Lakota empire was particularly disruptive for other tribes. After victory in one battle during the winter of 1837–38, Pawnee warriors returned to their villages with twenty captive Oglala women and children. Unfortunately, the captives had smallpox. Children in the Pawnee villages, who were already suffering from influenza and whooping cough, contracted the disease, and many died. The government began removing the weakened tribes to Indian Territory (later Oklahoma) or confining them to reservations.

In most locations where homesteaders staked claims, Native populations had already been removed or confined to reservations long before homesteaders showed up. In Kansas the government had dispossessed Indians of thirty-five million of Kansas's fifty-three million acres as early as 1850, well before homesteading started. In Nebraska the government dispossessed and transferred to the public domain thirty million of the state's forty-nine million acres before the Homestead Act was passed; only Nebraska's northwest corner remained legally in limbo.

We know from works like David Wishart's penetrating *An Unspeakable Sadness: The Dispossession of the Nebraska Indians* and William Unrau's *The Rise and Fall of Indian Country, 1825–1855* (about Kansas) that the dispossession process was unfair, venal, and tragic. In Kansas and Nebraska, however, it appears not to have been related in any significant way to homesteading. Similarly, in Colorado, the homesteading period came so long after the Indians lost their land that it is implausible to call homesteaders a prime cause. Denver alone had a population of 106,000 and was already a rail hub before any significant homesteading began in Colorado. In these areas a diverse collection of actors, especially mining companies, railroads, and speculators, pressed dispossession. Homesteading mostly occurred only long after whites had settled the issue of Native land titles.

In some places, however, especially Dakota Territory and Indian Territory, events were more compressed. There homesteading proceeded concurrently with dispossession. In 1876 Lakota, Arapaho, and Northern Cheyenne warriors won their victory at Little Bighorn in eastern Montana, but soon after, Indian resistance collapsed. In 1887 Congress passed the Dawes Act, which directed the government to assign allotments to individual Indian families, replacing communally held tribal lands. Would-be homesteaders and others pressed officials to open to homesteaders the "surplus" reservation land, that is, tribal land left over after all the individual Native allotments had been made.

In 1890 President Benjamin Harrison converted the Great Sioux Reservation into six much smaller reservations and authorized homesteading on the former reservation land thus freed up. In 1904 and again in 1909 President Theodore Roosevelt opened surplus Sioux land in South Dakota to homesteading. There homesteaders, mostly whites with some Black people, sometimes intermingled with the remaining Indian populations and became part of the process (legal or otherwise) of extinguishing Indian land claims.

The Homestead Act—"An Act to secure Homesteads to actual Settlers on the Public Domain"—allowed any person who was the head of a family, was twenty-one years old, and was either a U.S. citizen or had declared his or her intention to become a citizen to claim 160 acres of surveyed public land.

The question confronting the Thirty-Seventh Congress was Who among whites (and a smaller number of Blacks) would gain western land? Would public land be gobbled up by the bonanza ranchers, who were eager to run their cattle on the open range? Would it fall into the hands of land speculators, interested in profiting from what they expected to be rising land values? Or would it go directly to small farmers?

The land hoarders were everywhere. A bonanza rancher would typically own a relatively small piece of ground on which he built his ranch house, barns, and corrals. But then to graze his cattle he encroached on tens of thousands or even hundreds of thousands of acres of public open range. Ranchers and their wranglers became highly territorial over "their" grazing lands. Many even fenced the public land. Wranglers patrolled the fence lines to keep out intruders.

Bartlett Richards and William Comstock of the notorious Spade Ranch in western Nebraska controlled 500,000 acres, most of them public land. John B. Kendrick amassed control of 210,000 acres, which straddled northern Wyoming and south-eastern Montana. In western Nebraska alone, Reith & Barton ran 6,500 head of cattle; J. H. Bosler, 10,000 head; Creighton & Co., 6,000; J. M. Carey, 6,000; and J. W. Iliff, 7,000. Other ranchers ran similarly gigantic herds on public land.

Big speculators, too, got their hands in. William Scully purchased 71,750 acres in Marion and Dickinson counties, Kansas, and 63,987 acres in Gage and Nichols counties, Nebraska. He accumulated his empire mainly by buying up deeply discounted soldiers' warrants and agricultural college scrip. When he died in 1906 he owned 225,000 acres that he rented to 1,200 tenants. Other speculators built similarly huge empires.

Was this to be the future of the interior West—a land of few owners with enormous holdings? Or would the land go to the dirt farmers who wanted to own the land and actually settle on it? The many laws governing disbursement of public lands were complex and often pulled in different directions. The Homestead Act, with its emphasis on "actual settlers," said the land should go to the dirt farmers.

But the Homestead Act was just a law passed in Washington. For the homestead vision to become a reality, millions of would-be farmers would need to migrate west and file their claims. This was the drama to be played out over the next half-century.

It worked like this: an "entryman," or claimant, found a piece of surveyed but unclaimed public land, marked it with stakes, and scurried off to the local land office. He or she paid fourteen dollars in filing fees (equivalent to about $400 today). The entryman had to build a dwelling not less than ten by fourteen feet, cultivate at least ten acres, and reside on the land for five years. (Claimants had another option: after living on the claim for fourteen months, they could "commute," or purchase, their claims for $1.25 an acre, or twice that if the claim lay within a railroad grant.)

After the homesteader completed residency, he or she "proved up," or documented for the General Land Office (GLO) that the claimant had met all the law's requirements. The residency requirement ensured that only "actual settlers," and not speculators or land aggregators, would get the land. After the claimant proved up, the GLO then sent out a patent or land title. This completed the transfer of land from the public domain to the homesteader. The homesteader then owned his or her "free" land.

The law was amended several times, but it mostly remained true to the homesteading principle—free land for actual settlers. The Kinkaid Act (1904) authorized claims of 640 acres in an especially arid eight-million-acre region of western Nebraska. The Enlarged Homestead Act (1909) permitted 320-acre claims in most other areas of the drier West. Required residency was reduced from five years to three. The GLO made other changes in regulations. Some, like stricter proving-up procedures, tightened up the law against fraud. Others, like the special veterans' benefit, made the law more generous. But free land remained the centerpiece.

Homesteaders entered the Great Plains only after many white fortune-seekers had already passed through. First came the fur traders in the 1820s and 1830s, with their annual rendezvous and trading posts, the basis of John Jacob Astor's empire. Then, in the 1840s, came the early settlers heading up the Oregon Trail to what would become the states of Washington and Oregon. Others turned off at South Pass (Wyoming) to reach the rich lands of California. In 1847 Mormons made their arduous migration, many pulling handcarts, to settle around the Great Salt Lake.

In 1849 the massive wave of "forty-niners" passed through, hoping the tales of quick fortunes made in the goldfields were true. Other would-be miners heard of the enormous Comstock Lode silver strike in Nevada in 1858 or wanted to try their luck in the silver and gold mines in Colorado. The masses of migrants passing through Stephen Long's "Great American Desert" knew their dreams lay farther west. Few wanted to stay in the endless sea of grass. Only after the Civil War and passage of the Homestead Act did settlers begin focusing on the Great Plains.

In homesteading's first phase, from roughly 1868 to 1892, horse- or ox-drawn wagons and crowded homesteader trains passed every day through the gateway cities of Kansas City, St. Joseph, and Omaha. They carried streams of families arriving to begin their search for land. Between 1860 and 1890 Kansas's non-Indian population grew thirteen-fold, from 107,206 to 1,428,108. Nebraska topped that. During the same three decades its non-Indian population exploded thirty-six-fold, from 28,841 to 1,062,656. Homesteaders drove most of this growth. They soon filled up the eastern and central portions of Kansas and Nebraska and southeastern Dakota Territory.

In homesteading's second phase, stretching from the mid-1890s through the early 1920s, landseekers pushed farther west, north, and south. People searching for available land to homestead needed to go to the Dakotas, the eastern plains of Colorado, and newly opened Oklahoma. Between 1900 and 1920 North Dakota's non-Indian population doubled, from 319,146 to 646,872. Between 1890 and 1910 Oklahoma's non-Indian population ballooned eight-fold from 194,163 to 1,582,143.

After 1910 homesteaders shifted even farther west, to the western edge of the Great Plains, creating a homesteading boom in eastern Montana, eastern New Mexico, and Nebraska's sandhills. More claims were proved up between 1901 and 1920 than during any other period.

By the end of the 1920s homesteading was mostly over. Potential claimants found the lands then available unsuitable for farming, and they viewed farming itself as a less promising opportunity than jobs in cities. The farmers' hard times of the 1920s and then the disaster of the 1930s wiped out many who had started with such high hopes. But the homesteaders and their descendants had already left their mark on America.

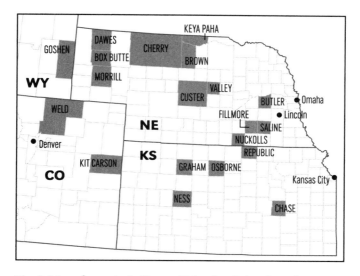

**Fig. 6.** Map of counties in Kansas, Nebraska, Colorado, and Wyoming mentioned in the text. Map by Katie Nieland.

# CHAPTER THREE

# Moving to the Land in the Nineteenth Century

They came to a living prairie that was a marvelous and alien place, disorienting to newcomers in its vastness. It had evolved over millennia to become not just grass but a complex organic system incorporating hundreds of species of grasses and forbs (broad-leaved, nonwoody plants). Early researchers, impressed by the prairie's toughness, made the radical suggestion that the prairie itself should be considered an organism, rather than the individual plants growing within it. The prairie created a natural stability and hardy persistence that invasive weeds could not penetrate so long as its vegetation was not torn up.

Each ecological niche, separated by miles or altitude or topography or season, hosted its own unique mixture of species. Each species took its turn in its ecosystem. Some emerged early in the growing season, reaching maturity before being crowded out by later arrivals. Others only grew to fullness late in the summer.

The seasons brought a changing profusion of color, spring showing the golden parsnip's yellow, the prairie phlox's bright pink and purple, New Jersey tea's white flowers, and the buffalo bean's abundance of violet purple. Summer followed with prairie clover's white and purple flowers; black-eyed Susans' bright yellows; tick trefoil's pink or rose-purple blossoms; wild licorice's white, cream, and pale yellow blooms; wild bergamot's showy pink and purple; and rosinweeds' big yellows, like small sunflowers.

And the grasses. The "big four" of big bluestem, little bluestem, Indian grass, and switchgrass dominated. But many others competed as well, including buffalo grass, needlegrass, salt grass, eastern gamagrass, western wheatgrass, blue grama, and many more. On the eastern edge, in places such as Beadle County, South Dakota, and Chase County, Kansas, the grasses grew as tall as the head of a man riding a horse. As settlers moved farther west, they found the grasses grew shorter. And in what was a nasty surprise to many homesteaders who tried to plow it, prairies stored three-quarters of their biomass underground in their deep, dense, and entwined root systems.

The prairie relied on its partners, the bison and prairie dogs, for crucial help. Millions of bison, intensely grazing in one area and then moving to the next, assisted the rotation of the grasses. Modern prairie restorers know that grazing is a crucial component of a healthy prairie. Today's most progressive cattle ranchers attempt to replicate the bison's grazing pattern with detailed "rotational grazing" schemes. So too, billions of prairie dogs churned up the soil, supporting their own niche ecosystems. Native peoples added fire, to which the prairie adapted and which it incorporated into its evolution as well.

By early fall, sparse rainfall and colder nights turned the prairie a desiccated brown, making its earlier profusion of color seem but a dream. It would wear its plain brown coat until it awoke again the next spring,

Most people had to think long and hard before deciding to make this strange place their home. They may have heard, or would soon learn, that the climate and soil were different from what most of them had known before. They couldn't depend on plentiful precipitation as they had back home in more humid regions. Periodic droughts withered their crops and wiped out their prospects. They faced hail, windstorms, blistering sun, prairie fires, dust storms, insect clouds that blotted out the sun, frosts that came too late in the spring and too early in the fall, and killing winter blizzards.

They knew they were signing up for years of unceasing toil, and they were putting themselves and their families at great risk. They would be taking a step that would likely change their lives forever.

They began dreaming about and fretting about homesteading long before they started their journey. They would be leaving behind everything familiar—their extended networks of relatives and friends and what years later most still referred to as "back home." They would put themselves beyond the means of easy communication—even mail and the telegraph would be in town, perhaps several hours travel from the farm. Returning for visits to the place they left behind would be expensive and further limited by the need for someone to stay home and tend the livestock. It was a lot to think about. Only the young entered into this adventure with a light heart and little worry about possible bad consequences.

E. D. Haney carefully considered whether to homestead before he made his decision. He served in an Indiana regiment during the Civil War and was discharged in Texas. He moved to Minnesota and Iowa and spent several years teaching and going to college. But he grew frustrated when his life didn't advance as quickly as he hoped. In the winter of 1870–71 he discussed homesteading possibilities with two Iowa veterans he knew, and they decided to try to get some of the free government land. He promised his fiancée he would send for her in two years.

The three men packed up and traveled west in a covered wagon pulled by a team of horses. When they arrived on the east bank of the Missouri River opposite Nebraska City, they were met by a gale wind so fierce it made the ferry crossing too dangerous. They waited for three days for the storm to blow itself out, and while waiting, they met two other ex-soldiers headed to Kansas to homestead. They decided to travel together. The five men arrived north of Belleville, in Republic County in central Kansas, just south of the Nebraska line, on April 28. After spending a couple of days looking for available land, they drove the twenty miles south to the Concordia land office to file their claims. They were now homesteaders.

Henry Burden traveled farther than most, socially as well as geographically, to claim his homestead. He had been born into slavery in Petersburg, Virginia, about 1840. When his owner took him to build fortifications for General Lee's army around Richmond, he slipped away to Union lines. He joined the United States Colored Troops, was mustered out when the war ended, traveled to Wisconsin and then on to Lincoln, Nebraska. He worked for a time at Atwood House, a fancy Lincoln hotel, but he had a bigger ambition: *to own land*. He homesteaded in Saline County, Nebraska, where he claimed eighty acres. He, too, had become a homesteader.

Knudt Fredrikson and his older brother Ole crossed the ocean to homestead. They left Norway, with its beautiful mountains, breathtaking fiords, and mostly democratic government because Norwegian farmers found it difficult to make a living. Many families rented their farms, and those who owned their land tended to own only small patches, five acres or so, of rocky ground. Younger sons could not expect to inherit even that. Faced with such dim prospects at home and hearing about the almost inconceivable promise of 160 acres of free, fertile land, Knudt and Ole decided to emigrate.

After their transatlantic crossing and the long overland journey, they arrived in eastern Dakota Territory. Ole filed a 160-acre homestead claim on the flat terrain and rich soil of Nelson County in 1885, and Knudt did the same in 1891.

Some homesteaders put down roots near others who shared their culture. Czech migrants settled in a cluster around Wilber in Saline County, Nebraska, where some homesteaded; others purchased land. Black migrants from Lexington, Kentucky, filed homesteads together at Nicodemus in Graham County, Kansas. Even with familiar neighbors, however, they found themselves cut off from most of what they knew. And for some, like the flood of young men who left Norway for North Dakota, or the Germans from Russia who settled around Sutton in Clay County, Nebraska, returning home was almost inconceivable. For most claimants, homesteading was a one-way ticket.

They traveled to their new homesteads in a variety of conveyances. Some walked. Charles Swanson, a Swedish immigrant, came to the Middle Loup valley in Custer County, Nebraska, in 1884. Most of the good land had already been claimed, but he found a quarter section that looked promising. He walked the 102 miles back to the Grand Island land office to file his claim. He returned to his homestead by way of Ord, where he bought a hatchet, a spade, and a red blanket. With that equipment on his back and three dollars and thirty-five cents in his pocket, Swanson walked to his claim to begin farming.

The most common conveyance was the prairie schooner—a light but sturdy wagon with a canvas top cover. It was an adaptation of the heavier Conestoga wagon, which was the freighter of its day. The Conestoga had a ten-foot-by-four-foot bed, with four-foot-high sideboards and four-inch-wide wheels. It could carry six tons of cargo. But its weight meant that when loaded it required four or even five teams of oxen to pull it. Hauling that much weight, drivers mainly stuck to well-worn trails or cart paths.

**Fig. 7.** Prairie schooner, the homesteaders' most common means of conveyance during phase one of homesteading. Drawing by Adam Edwards Mayhew.

The prairie schooner, by contrast, was lighter—designed to carry only one family and able to haul one ton of freight. Its bed was eight feet by four feet, with two-foot-high sidewalls. It had narrower wheels and could be pulled by one or two teams of horses or oxen. Families could drive schooners across the raw prairie following no trail at all. Drivers of the schooners learned from the freighters to tar the seams between the boards in the box. That way the family's clothes and barrels of flour stayed dry when they crossed a river.

Many in Wisconsin and Missouri and Indiana loaded all their household goods and farm machinery in prairie schooners and headed west. William Downey and his wife left Kalamazoo, Michigan, in a schooner, traveling with three other families. They were six weeks on the journey, stopping Sundays in deference to Downey's strict religious beliefs. Downey homesteaded in Fillmore County, Nebraska, in 1872.

Robert Anderson, a freedman, bought a wagon and team in Iowa in 1870. He obtained a contract to carry a freight load to

Lincoln, paying for that part of his trip. He then homesteaded in Butler and Lancaster counties in eastern Nebraska. Some families traveled by train as far as they could, and then switched to wagons pulled by teams of horses or oxen.

When the weather turned cold, some travelers set up stoves right in the wagons to keep themselves warm. Stillman Gates, living in Iowa, went to Nebraska to scout out the opportunities. Liking what he saw, in April 1882 he filed a homestead claim. He then returned to Iowa to get his wife and children. But his wife was sickly and couldn't withstand difficult travel; so Gates built a six-by-sixteen-foot house right on top of his wagon wheels. He placed a small stove in the center for cooking and to keep her warm. He hitched four horses to pull it, and they made their way to his Custer County homestead.

The last miles traveled—they might be four or forty across a roadless prairie—were nearly always the hardest, the trip made in a wagon or on foot. Most claimants moved into raw lands, bisected only by game trails or no trails at all. They deposited their goods, set up a tent or other temporary shelter, and got to work.

Settlers flowed into all parts of Nebraska, Kansas, and eastern Dakota Territory—immigrants, native-born farmers grown tired of renting ground in Iowa or Indiana or who had failed in Virginia, people down on their luck, or dreamers from New York or Connecticut who just wanted a better chance at life than they had seen so far.

All homesteaders, despite their great diversity as individuals, faced common challenges. To begin and succeed at homesteading, they needed to find and file on land, build a shelter, find a water supply, plow ("break") the tough prairie sod, get a first crop in, and survive both the withering summer sun and the frigid winters. Many also had to deal with debilitating stress, anxiety, loneliness, and depression. Most felt a surge of pride when they finally received patents and knew they owned land.

The land seeker's first problem was to find good land to claim. Initial settlers in a region might have many choices, but latecomers found that rural neighborhoods filled up quickly once word got around that land was available. Custer County, Nebraska, filled up between 1870 and 1885, and while the county still contained some public land afterward, it was of inferior quality for farming.

Claimants faced an additional problem: how to tell good land from bad. Many had little or no farming experience, so they couldn't know whether the land they had chosen would produce bountiful crops or not. Land with lush-looking grasses and beautiful vistas might nonetheless be waterlogged or have thin, alkaline soils or other problems. Chris Bartsch, a Kansas homesteader, claimed bad land. By the time he arrived in Osborne County, all the good land had already been filed on, so he and his wife and children struggled to extract a living from their inferior claim.

William Newton ("Newt") Anderson and his wife Hettie Lee Anderson were married in Carroll County, Missouri, in 1875. Newt was young and without any business training, but he found a position where he was being trained as a bookkeeper. He and Hettie were making modest progress in life. Then Newt fell prey to what Hettie called "this excitement that sprung up in that part of the country over going to Nebraska to homestead government land."

Newt joined a group of older, responsible men led by a Dr. Rosenburg, who went west to investigate and find a suitable place for friends and neighbors to settle. They explored Keya Paha County, Nebraska, up near the Dakota line. It seemed promising country, though snow blanketed the ground when the men arrived, making it hard to assess its soil quality. Newt was impressed with its beauty and immediately filed a homestead claim. It was the naive young man's first big mistake.

Newt was dismayed to learn that the other men decided not to file in Keya Paha. In fact, none of Newt's and Hettie's neighbors from back home—whom they had counted on to settle near them—chose to go to Keya Paha either. Newt had by then used up his right to claim a homestead. He was unwilling to give up his opportunity to own land, so he and Hettie moved to the claim. But few other settlers located nearby, and the Andersons found it to be a lonely spot.

Worse, their ground was poor farming land. Newt had chosen bad land, and his poor choice handicapped his and Hettie's homesteading venture. They struggled for years to make the farm support them. But a person only had one chance to make a claim, so when, like Newt, claimants made bad choices, they were stuck with them.

People learned where land was available and maybe got advice on whether it was good farming country through both formal and informal mechanisms. Undoubtedly more important were the informal ones. Claimants heard news from relatives who preceded them, friends who wrote to them, and strangers in casual conversations. But the accuracy of the information gleaned through advice, tips, gossip, and rumors was highly variable. People giving out information sometimes had their own agendas or simply passed on bad intelligence.

Those who caught homesteading fever were also subjected to a flood of information and misinformation from agents and promoters. The railroads encouraged settlement on government lands because it would increase their freight traffic. And they were eager to sell their own acres, obtained through massive government grants, to convert their land into cash.

Railroads companies advertised widely to woo land seekers. The Kansas City, Lawrence, and Southern Railway promoted settlement on 5.8 million acres in Kansas. Some lines even hired agents abroad to encourage immigration among Czechs, Germans, Austrians, and others. They published pamphlets extolling the beauty and fertility of the lands available, but they passed over in silence the droughts, bitter winters, and locusts. Land companies, land agents, land "lawyers" (rules were lax about who could claim to be an attorney), and assorted hangers-on who lived on land sales contributed misinformation as well.

These groups issued a blizzard of unreliable and shameless broadsheets, flyers, and booklets promoting emigration and settlement. States and towns joined in, setting up immigration bureaus to encourage newcomers to settle in their jurisdictions.

The Nebraska legislature, in 1870, created the state Board of Immigration to attract new residents. It promoted settlement on fifty million acres in "The Garden of the West." In 1873 J. H. Noteware, Nebraska's state superintendent of immigration, published a lengthy brochure titled "The State of Nebraska, Illustrated by a New and Authentic Map, Accompanied by Some Statements in Answer to the Following Queries: Where Is It? What Is It? What Shall It Become? When Shall These Things Be?"

The quality of Noteware's promotions may perhaps be judged by his answer to the question, Where Is It? He informed readers that "Nebraska is eminently fit to be where it is, on the natural highway of this nation and of all nations, where the traveling and trading world can see and enjoy it without going out of their way." Nebraska was not some remote outpost—it was right there at the center of the world's thoroughfare!

Private groups promoted migration to the land as well. In 1896 the Kansas Immigration and Information Association published "A Kansas Souvenir: A Book of Information Relative to the Moral, Educational, Agricultural, Commercial, Manufacturing, and Mining Interests of the State." The authors condemned

**Fig. 8.** Railroad promotional advertisement for Kansas land, circa 1880s. Permission of the Kansas State Historical Society.

"censorious scoffers" who "intimated that the [typical Kansan] unduly vaunteth himself; that he brags . . . and is given to bounce, tall talk, and magniloquence." That was slander—the Kansan was, the authors insisted, modest and self-effacing.

To set the record straight, the Immigration Association noted that to live in Kansas meant being "a denizen of a State that surpasses all other communities as Niagara excels all other cataracts, as the sun transcends all other luminaries." No tall talk here!

Edwin Curley reported for *The Field, The Farm, The Garden: The Country Gentleman's Newspaper*, a London sheet which proclaimed itself to be Britain's second-most popular publication. Curley came to Nebraska in 1872 to report on all the excitement surrounding "free land." He wrote several long articles for *The Field* and afterward published a handsome red-covered volume called *Nebraska: Its Advantages, Resources, and Drawbacks*. The book was an immediate bestseller in both New York and London. Migrants likely benefited from his extensive discussion of soils, rainfall, rivers, and streams and from his detailed maps.

Curley was enthusiastic about all the opportunities open to enterprising men in "the Far West." Although Nebraska's population was then fewer than three hundred thousand, it was growing rapidly. Curley used detailed charts and extrapolations to project that the state's population would grow to 6.8 million by 1940, equaling London. (His forecast was slightly off: Nebraska's homesteader-driven growth pushed its population past one million by 1890, but when homesteading stopped, so did population growth. The state failed to reach even two million by 2020.)

Travelers themselves poured out a steady stream of helpful guides. Frances Fulton's brother, C. T. Fulton, organized a colony from Bradford, Pennsylvania, to settle in Nebraska. Frances published an informative if chatty report on her family's homesteading experience in Brown County. She called it "To and Through Nebraska by a Pennsylvania Girl." She modestly introduced it as "This Little Work, which claims no merit but Truth."

Out of all this information and misinformation, homesteaders mostly had to figure out for themselves where to settle. E. D. Haney and the Civil War veterans he traveled with heard stories of homesteading land available in north-central Kansas and went to Republic County investigate. They found the stories were true and filed claims near one another.

Henry Burden, the freedman and former Union soldier, must have heard many tales of available land while working at Atwood House in Lincoln. Growing up in slavery left him illiterate, but he had a bright intelligence and was keenly oriented to the new opportunities. He seemed to know exactly where to go south of Pleasant Hill in Saline County to locate an eighty-acre claim. He filed his papers in April 1870.

Later that same year Burden filed a second claim on eighty acres in nearby Polk County, using the "additional soldier entry" provision that Congress had passed just that year. Burden, illiterate and isolated on his claim, somehow heard about the new benefit within months of Congress passing it. How could he have learned about the new law? His second filing demonstrated the astonishing effectiveness of informal information networks.

Once on a claim, the homesteader turned to his or her first job, constructing a dwelling. Homesteaders and their families needed shelter at all times of the year, and they also needed to demonstrate during proving up that they had built a dwelling at least ten by fourteen feet in size. For the first few weeks or months, especially if they were summer months, the homesteading family might live in the wagon that carried them out or in tents or some other temporary shelter while constructing more permanent quarters.

In March 1872, in Skyler County, Illinois, John and Martha David loaded their children and a few household goods, including a small cookstove and iron boiler, into a covered wagon pulled by two small mules. Several David relatives accompanied them in their own wagons. After a month traveling, the party arrived in Harlan County, Nebraska, where they filed homestead and timber culture claims. They lived in their wagons while the men set to work building their dwellings and digging a well.

The most primitive longer-term dwelling was the dugout, much used in the 1870s and 1880s. It came in two versions. If there was a convenient hill or ravine on the claim, the homesteader dug into its side, using the earth itself for three walls, roof, and floor. He tucked the beds into the darker recess excavated at the back. Many builders added a sod front room extending out from the hill, with a door and perhaps a window.

If no hill was available, the builders dug down. Early homesteaders at Nicodemus started by digging out a hole, at least ten by fourteen feet wide and three or four feet deep. They cut through the mass of tangled prairie roots. Then they cut sod into usable strips to build up the side walls to three or four feet above ground. They added cottonwood or hackberry boughs cut at a riverbank as the rafters. They roofed the squat half-dugout, half-sod home with sod, dirt, and other material.

The chief, and perhaps only, advantage of the dugout was that it was cheap. Oscar Babcock was a Baptist minister who preached at North Loup in Valley County, Nebraska. He constructed a fourteen-foot-square dugout in 1872. He added up the cost of the purchased items: one ten-inch-by-twelve-inch window, lumber for his door, a latch, a stovepipe, and nails. Total cost: $2.78 ½.

**Fig. 9.** Sod dugout with sod front wall and sod roof on the South Loup River, Custer County, Nebraska, 1892. Photo by Solomon Butcher. Permission of History Nebraska.

Dugouts were dark and dirty. In summer they attracted snakes, flies, and other critters. When it rained the roof often leaked. Residents usually found it necessary to dig a small trench down the middle of the floor to drain away the water seeping in. But on a treeless plain, a dugout provided relief from the enfeebling summer sun and frostbite of winter. Still, most inhabitants disliked living in a hole in the ground, both for its inconvenience and its ignominy.

Sod houses were a much better, though more expensive, choice. The sod was free, except for the back-breaking work of cutting and hauling it. Typically, builders also used some purchased boards and windows. To get the sod, a homesteader would find a place where the prairie grasses grew especially lush and entangled. He might need a half-acre to gather enough sod to construct a ten-foot-by-fourteen-foot house. Several men, working together, cut or carefully plowed the sod, turning it over without breaking it up. They took a spade and chopped it into three-foot bricks. If they had a horse and stoneboat (a kind of sled) available, they would haul the sod to the house site; if not, they had to carry the heavy bricks themselves.

The men, who sometimes included a hired sod mason, laid the sod in courses, like bricks. They marked out the foundation with the first course. Then they laid subsequent courses on the first, staggering the joints to increase wall strength. Every third or fourth course they placed perpendicular to the one below it to increase stability. Boards were scarce and expensive, so many families made do with dirt floors and a roof constructed out of tree boughs overlaid with sod.

At some cost but vast benefit, families could use lumber for the floor and roof. Konrad Gebhart of St. Joseph, Missouri, went west in 1872 in a prairie schooner—he owned one horse in the team, another man owned the other horse, and a third man owned the wagon. He explored homestead possibilities in Custer County, Nebraska, on that trip and returned in 1874 to settle.

Four years later Gebhart brought his family out, building a half-dugout, half-sod house. For the roof, he put up a ridge pole, then pole rafters running down to the top of the walls, all covered by plum brush, hay, and dirt, making the roof about a foot thick. Gebhart considered himself a generous spender, so to please his wife, he splurged and bought boards for the floor. But they discovered that, when it rained, the roof leaked. Moreover, it acted like a sponge, and water kept dripping, even a day after the rain ended. Gebhart's wife often wished he had put the boards on the roof instead of the floor.

Wilber Speer, out from Wisconsin, built a sod house for his family on their Custer County, Nebraska, claim. As a special treat for his wife, he put in a board floor. They could move out of their dugout, which she hated, and she was delighted with how easily she could clean the new floor. But the first time it rained, their sod and brush roof leaked badly, and she and her husband decided they'd rather put the floorboards on the roof. Lost the nice floor but kept dry.

Four men could construct a substantial sod house in three or four days. The family typically stockpiled, beforehand, any boards needed to make window frames and the door. When all was ready, the builders, neighbors, or hired workers showed up. Hired men typically charged about fifty dollars (roughly $1,500.00 in today's money) to build a house.

Many families started by constructing a ten-by-fourteen-foot sod house, the minimum size needed for proving up. But over time, as the family accumulated some savings or more children arrived, they built larger and more complex buildings. Some added a separate chamber to shelter the stock during the coldest part of winter. Some built sod barns. Some added a lean-to for a kitchen. Some added bedrooms. In Nicodemus, Myers House and Union House, two early "hotels," were really just sod houses, enlarged, with a couple of guest rooms added.

Families typically constructed a root cellar along with the sod house. They dug six or eight feet down, saving the excavated dirt to build up the ground around it. The builder then roofed over the hole and piled dirt on top. In my grandparents' soddy, the cellar was beneath the house, and everything stored in it sat on the dirt floor. Cellars usually remained warm enough in winter to keep the stored jars of canned tomatoes and beans from freezing and cool enough in summer to prevent partially cured meats from spoiling.

Some homesteaders, when lumber was available and they had money to pay for it, built frame houses right away. James Dolan, a veteran of the 18th Iowa regiment, came out on the train to Lincoln, Nebraska, on February 1, 1871, then traveled by stagecoach to Crete, and then walked to Fillmore County, Nebraska. He found an acceptable claim and returned to Lincoln to file on it. On April 13 he purchased lumber in Lincoln for his house. He paid forty-five dollars for the boards, one window, and one door. He also bought some hardware and nails. He hired a drayman who hauled the single wagonload of building materials to his claim for twelve dollars. He built the twelve-by-fourteen-foot house himself. In total, Dolan's house with a board roof cost sixty-five dollars.

Many who lived in dugouts or soddies moved out of them as soon as they could afford to build a proper frame house. William Dyer migrated from England in 1871 and homesteaded eighty acres in Fillmore County, Nebraska, in 1874. He built a dugout and sod house, to which he brought his wife and child. They lived in it until 1880, when he built a frame house. Unfortunately, his wife died that same year, likely in childbirth, leaving Dyer with five small children to raise in his new house.

More affluent homesteaders built substantial frame houses, like a produce box turned on its end, two stories tall enclosing four rooms; it had a porch running the full length of the front and perhaps a small lean-to at the rear. Across the Great Plains landscape today we often see these now-abandoned and collapsing homesteaders' homes, with roofs caving in and fringed by a line of scraggly trees. They stand as outposts to a world left behind.

Most homesteaders quickly turned to a second pressing task: finding water. They needed water for drinking and household use and also for the animals. On the semiarid plain, they needed to water their vegetable gardens to make them bloom. If they planted fruit trees, they needed to water them. Some settlers filed claims along streams or rivers, easing the problem of getting water. But even streams and creeks that overflowed in spring might dry to a trickle or less by late summer.

Most homesteaders did not have easy access to a year-round stream and struggled to find a reliable source of water. Some hauled water from the nearest river or pond or a neighbor's well. Women and children typically took on this chore, while the men worked in the field. Thor and Gjertru Birkelo, on their Williams County, North Dakota, homestead, had no stream, so they drew water from a deep slough a mile south of their house and hauled it home. But water is heavy, and it tired those who filled and hauled the barrels. They risked injury wrestling the heavy barrels on and off a wagon. And even the livestock, pulling a loaded water wagon, tired quickly.

Fetching water seemed a never-ending task. One of its most pernicious effects was that it created a mentality of water scarcity, so family members constantly worried about using too much water.

Homesteaders found the best answer was having a well. A well that produced an adequate flow of sweet-tasting water, and which was located near the house or barn, saved many, many hours of labor. And it eliminated the anxiety over "wasting" water. Settlers with wells considered themselves lucky.

In the nineteenth century homesteaders dug their own wells or hired professional well diggers to do it. Either way, most wells were dug by hand. One man worked at the bottom of the hole, digging and filling a bucket while his mates on the surface hauled up the fill and dumped it.

A digger found himself excavating in a confined space in dim light, which became even dimmer as the hole went deeper. He especially struggled when he struck a large rock. He had to break the rock up before the pieces could be lugged to the top. This was dangerous and uncertain work. The loaded pail going up to be dumped could dislodge stones in the wall, which could then come crashing on his head. Even worse, he was at risk of being buried alive by cave-ins of the gravel and sand sidewalls.

The depth of the water table across the Great Plains varied enormously. In some places like the Nebraska sandhills, settlers could drive a pipe into the ground and strike water at ten or fifteen feet. But more commonly, homesteaders only struck water at thirty or forty feet, and it was not unheard of to have to go down two hundred feet or more. It seemed a chancy gamble, because finding water was so random—one family might strike a good flow at twenty feet, while their neighbors got no water until eighty feet. And worst of all, their digging might produce a well that came up completely dry.

Wiley B. Wright homesteaded with his family in 1873 in Nuckolls County, Nebraska. The first winter he dug a well with the help of some men. They hauled the excavated fill to the surface using a windlass. The man digging at the bottom of the hole loosened dirt and filled the bucket with it. Then the men up top turned a cylinder, winding the rope around it and pulling up the bucket. Using the same mechanism, they lowered stone to the man at the bottom, who walled up the bottom fifteen feet of the hole. Wright found that the top part of his hole did not cave in so long as he didn't let surface water run into the well. They struck water at sixty-three feet.

When they finished the well, they repurposed the windlass to draw up pails of water. But a well that deep made the rope-and-water-filled bucket very heavy—the children needed to turn handles on both ends of the cylinder to crank it up.

Because wells were difficult and expensive to dig, homesteaders with wells tended to share their water, just as they often shared expensive farm implements. Jim Ankeny and George Cummings homesteaded adjacent parcels in Custer County, Nebraska. They decided to dig a well on the boundary between their two places. The well produced a good flow, so they allowed many others to haul water from the well. The almost universal ethic was that a well owner never charged for the water.

Charles Swanson, the Swede who walked to Grand Island and back to file his claim, normally drew his family's water from a pond. But when the weather turned warm, the pond water looked the color of tea and every bucket included a dozen half-inch wrigglers. So in summer the Swansons switched to the Ankeny-Cummings well, whose water was usually clear and tasted good.

One day people found that the water in the Ankeny-Cummings well had turned "riley," or turbid. Someone needed to go down and find out what the problem was. The well was 230 feet deep, about the same depth as a twenty-story building is high. No one else volunteered, so Cummings said he would go down the hole himself. He tied a loop in a rope which he used for a seat, and some men up top slowly lowered him down. When he was almost at the bottom, the well caved in.

The men up top sent for a professional well digger. Using his superior gear, this man went down to assess the situation, and when he came back out, he devised a rescue plan with the rest of the men. They managed to loop a rope around Cummings's body. By pulling on that rope and on the original rope Cummings had used as a seat, they hauled him up. But he was badly injured, and he died a few days later.

Besides cave-ins, foul air in a well posed another mortal danger. Variously called "coal gas" or "damps," the well collected methane, carbon dioxide, nitrogen, and hydrogen sulfide at the bottom, because those gasses are heavier than normal air. A Scotsman named McKinley was digging a well in 1870 near Belleville, in Republic County, Kansas. He filled his bucket with the stones and gravel he had excavated at the bottom. Then, having no helpers, he carried the bucket up his rope ladder himself to dump it at the top. On Saturday, he reached forty feet and then stopped for the weekend.

On Monday he resumed digging. When he failed to come back to the house for lunch, his wife went to find him. She saw him lying prostrate at the bottom of the well. She assumed he had fallen, and she put out the call for help. While waiting for the neighborhood men to gather, she climbed down the rope ladder to tend to her husband.

The men arrived and found her lying prostrate at the bottom of the well alongside her husband. The men got them out, but both had suffocated and were dead.

The men surmised that when McKinley had worked the previous week, he went up and down the ladder to carry the dirt out. His movements stirred up the air, causing it to circulate and lifting the damps out of the well. But over the weekend, the killing gas had collected at the bottom. On Monday when he returned, the gas suffocated both McKinley and his wife.

Undoubtedly the most famous well accident involved Jules Sandoz, famous because his daughter, the author Mari Sandoz, wrote about it in her celebrated book, *Old Jules*. Jules Sandoz was a Swiss immigrant who filed homestead and Kinkaid (640-acre) claims in Sheridan County, Nebraska. He was a hunter, postmaster, land locator, fighter, and relentless bane to his enemies. He beat his wives. He was handy with his rifle and refused to be intimidated by the aggrandizing ranchers and their trigger-happy wranglers.

Soon after he came to western Nebraska, Jules decided to dig a well on his claim. He arranged with two other young Swiss immigrants, Paul Nicolet and Jules Tissot, to help him dig the well in exchange for assisting them in filing land claims for themselves. The men joked around and tried to outdo each other with tales of the pranks they had pulled on others.

Sandoz worked at the bottom of the well, filling a bucket with dirt. Nicolet and Tissot pulled it to the top and emptied it. Sometimes the men at the top would wave a coat over the narrow hole to panic Sandoz, or they would make the filled bucket dance over his head as the frightened Sandoz shouted with alarm and anger.

Finally they struck water, and the next day they worked to clean out the well and finish up. When the final bucket of mud was raised and dumped, Nicolet and Tissot could not resist pulling a last gag on Sandoz. As they were pulling him up, they jerked the rope several times, causing him to bob up and down crazily in the well, twisting and falling, and then jolting to a stop. Nicolet and Tissot laughed and laughed as Sandoz cursed at them. At some point the frayed rope broke, sending Sandoz crashing to the bottom. He smashed his ankle bones.

Sandoz was a hundred miles from a hospital and fretful that if he didn't file on his land, claim jumpers would get it. So he tried to tough it out with morphine and wine. His friends departed to get help and file on their own land.

His foot swelled up, and no help came. In desperation and expecting to die, Sandoz crawled out to a prairie trail occasionally used by soldiers. He was in luck. Some troopers happened by and found him, unconscious and with one of his ankles swollen to the size of a bucket. They carted him to Fort Robinson. He recovered consciousness, though he was still woozy.

The post surgeon, Dr. Walter Reed, told him he needed to amputate the foot to save Sandoz's life. Jules, in his emaciated, fevered state glared at the doctor. "You cut my foot off, doctor, and I shoot you so dead you stink before you hit the ground."

Walter Reed backed away, and Sandoz spent the next several months in the hospital. He endured agonizing pain only somewhat relieved by morphine. But to the astonishment of the troops at the fort, all of whom by then knew his story, he survived. Ever after, however, he walked with a severe limp and enduring pain.

Water on the semiarid plains was a precious, life-giving commodity. When homesteaders had it in abundance, or at least in adequate supply, water made their gardens flourish and their cows give plentiful milk. But when it was scant or disappeared altogether, it compromised life itself. Homesteaders made big sacrifices to find it.

# CHAPTER FOUR

# Settling In in the Nineteenth Century

When the initial tasks of locating land, filing the claim, building a shelter, and finding water were completed, homesteaders turned to their longer-term challenge: figuring out how to make their patches of prairie into productive farms.

The plan seemed obvious: plow the prairie grasses under to make fields, plant wheat or corn (or rye, oats, barley, flax, sorghum, or potatoes), harvest your crop, haul it to the elevator, and take home the cash. In the meantime, grow your own food, make your own clothes, and purchase as little as possible. The reality was more complicated.

Homesteaders struggled with "breaking" the tangled roots of prairie sod. While buffalo grass sent its roots down only three feet, needlegrass roots might go down sixteen feet. With stringy roots tangled and interwoven, some shallow and others deep, prairie sod presented a tough barrier to cut through. Settlers needed a special breaking plow that cut deep into the earth, sliced off the roots, turned the sod over, and exposed the roots to the sun.

The tough sod meant that homesteaders needed tremendous pulling power to move the plow through the earth. Henry Eberstein, after being mustered out of the First Michigan Cavalry, homesteaded in Fillmore County, Nebraska, in 1870. He and his two brothers broke his land by hitching their twenty-four-inch breaking plow to *five yoke* of oxen. Isaac Merchant, a homesteader in Custer County, Nebraska, sold his mule team so he could buy oxen, better for breaking.

In 1871 James Dolan of Fillmore County, Nebraska, paid $135 for a yoke of oxen and $29 for a small breaking plow that made a twelve-inch furrow. But most homesteaders found that to avoid overtaxing the animals, several yokes of oxen or teams of horses worked better. Dr. W. A. Jones, on his homestead at the African American colony of Dearfield, Colorado, harnessed three and sometimes six horses, three abreast. Oscar Micheaux, on his Gregory and Tripp County, South Dakota, homesteads, yoked six teams of horses, astonishing neighbors with his ability to control that many animals by himself.

Newt Anderson struggled to get his ground broken on his Keya Paya homestead. After a year he had managed to put in ten acres of wheat and five of oats, and he also planted two and a half bushels of potatoes. When Newt's mule died, he was forced to make a deal with a neighbor, a Mr. Vessey. Anderson agreed to plow Vessey's ground using Vessey's team, and in return, Newt could use the team to work his own fields. But Anderson had a lot of work to do at home, and he lamented that if his mule had lived, he could have been working his own farm instead of Vessey's.

Breaking required the plowman to constantly press down on the plow to keep the blade from popping up out of the dirt. (One advantage of the wheeled riding plow that came along later was that the operator's body weight helped keep the blade in the ground.) Men found that working the plow and simultaneously driving the oxen or horses was extremely exhausting. When it could be arranged, a two-man team went better. One managed the animals and the other worked the plow. But either way, when the plow hit a big rock, it sent a bone-jarring jolt right through men and animals alike.

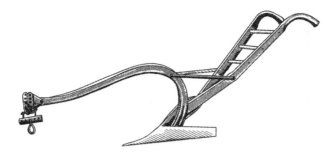

**Fig. 10.** Steel-bladed breaking plow. Drawing by Adam Edwards Mayhew.

Most homesteaders were poor and could not afford the special plow and the teams of oxen or horses to power it. When William and Sarah Athey arrived in the Middle Loup country in Custer County, Nebraska, in 1883, they owned only the team of horses that had pulled their wagon loaded with household goods. They had six dollars in cash. Randall Sargent, who homesteaded in Custer County in 1882, didn't own a plow, so he set to work and fashioned one out of the trunk of a water elm. It worked well enough that he and his brother made several for neighbors too. Still, it must have been vastly inferior to a steel-bladed plow.

Ordinary homesteaders wouldn't have needed multiple teams after the breaking was finished or wanted to shoulder their maintenance cost. So they made do, poorly, with borrowed plows and single horses or yokes of oxen. Or they shared the plow and team.

James R. Lang came out in 1874 from Indiana to homestead in Nebraska with his family. Temporarily leaving his wife and children in Grand Island, he ventured northwest until he found an unclaimed tract straddling the border between Sherman and Custer counties. It contained trees growing on part of it, flat land for fields, and access to water. He borrowed a team and breaking plow from a nearby settler, a complete stranger, and broke some acres. He then fetched his family and returned to break more acres.

Settlers at the Nicodemus colony in 1877 initially had only a couple of teams to share among seventy or so families. Colonists wanted to share because thriving neighbors helped everyone, but even so, many families lacked access to a team and plow. So, they dug by hand. Thorton Williams spaded up a big garden in his first spring, and he and his wife Elvira planted enough vegetables to carry them through the winter. By 1880 Nicodemus homesteaders owned sixteen sturdy teams and plows, which eased the problem but still meant they had to share.

Some settlers hired others to do their breaking. But it was a vicious cycle—they needed cash to hire someone to break the sod, but they needed the sod broken to grow crops to get the cash to pay the plow man. It drove settlers to take off-farm jobs. James Dolan unloaded lumber in Crete for the Burlington Railroad, receiving a dollar for each carload he unloaded. He used his wages to have his land broken. Sometimes settlers traded the labor of breaking others' fields for help with breaking their own. Many solved the cycle by going into debt.

Charles Swanson, the Swedish immigrant, got a job at sixteen dollars a month and saved his first two months' wages to pay a man to break a few acres on his claim. The following spring he bought a yoke of cattle on time since he didn't have money to pay for them. That summer he broke more of his own land, and he also plowed some prairie for other settlers, earning enough to pay for the team. He could break about two acres a day.

Christian Kobe, a German immigrant who homesteaded in York County, Nebraska, in 1870, owned two yoke of oxen. To supplement the meager income he earned from selling his own crops, he worked for several years breaking prairie for other settlers. He charged four dollars per acre.

Once the carpet of sod was broken, homesteaders knew they faced years of toil and struggle to turn the ground into productive fields. Usually they didn't harvest much of a crop the first year or two, draining their savings and driving many into debt.

Like most owners of small family-run businesses, homesteaders found the tasks awaiting them around the farm to be endless. They could always see something more that needed to be done. Because they lived on such slim margins, they worried that not doing that last job might mean the difference between having a successful year or not.

The reason they felt so stressed was clearly revealed in a 1968 study by an agricultural economist at the University of Missouri named Robert Finley. Finley tried to recreate the circumstances of Kansas and Nebraska homesteaders in the 1870s and 1880s by imagining a typical or "representative" farmer, which he then studied. Finley assumed that his representative farmer worked a 160-acre farm using then-available agricultural technology. For this homesteader Finley meticulously constructed a "time budget," measuring, month by month, how many hours it took for the homesteader to complete his tasks. Not surprisingly, from November through February, there were relatively few chores, and the settler had plenty of time to complete them.

But from March through October the homesteader faced heavy demands on his time. He faced peak demands from April to May and from July to August, a workload that would have crushed many farmers. One problem was that the farmer lost days of work when it rained—the moisture, so desired to make the crops thrive, also made the fields too wet to be workable. Finley employed weather data to show that farmers, on average, lost twelve working days each month during May, June, and July and ten days in August. As a result of this and other factors, farmers faced a huge labor shortage: the crops required many more days of labor than one homesteader could provide.

In April the farmer had a maximum of twenty-two days available to work, but tending his crops required between thirty and forty-five person-days of labor. In July he had nineteen days when the fields were dry enough to work, but he needed twenty-nine or thirty days to complete all the work. In August he could get into the fields twenty-one days, but the work to be done required between twenty-eight and thirty-seven days.

Finley's analysis covered only the labor required for field crops—corn, wheat, oats, and native hay. Not included, but certainly essential for the survival of most farms, was the labor devoted to taking care of livestock and poultry (milking, processing milk and cream, butchering hogs, and preserving the meat), tending the vegetable garden, hauling water, building and restringing fences, maintaining buildings, repairing equipment, and many other tasks. The wife (if the man was married) did some of these chores. Some could be put off to the less busy months, but most could not. They added to the farm's labor demands even beyond what Finley calculated.

A homesteader could close his big labor deficit in several ways, none good. One was that, if he had a wife and children, they could help in the fields, but that meant some of their own work didn't get done. Only older children, twelve and up, worked effectively in the field, whereas even young children were highly helpful in watering the livestock, collecting eggs, milking, and watching younger siblings.

And the wife's own work was crucial for the family's survival, so taking her away from it to work in the fields likely meant skimping elsewhere. She typically planted, watered, weeded, and harvested the vegetable garden. She preserved vegetables from the garden and fruit from the orchard for winter consumption. She gathered wild berries. She made and mended clothes.

she prepared meals, she fed and looked after the chickens and hogs, and she likely milked the cows or at least supervised her children doing it and then separated the cream and churned the butter. She sold eggs and butter and perhaps preserves, adding a crucial cash margin when field crops did poorly or prices were low.

A wife's work was the centerpiece of the family's strategy of buying as little as possible. The importance of her work could be seen in the privations endured by homesteading men who lacked wives. Taking the wife away from her own chores to help in the fields was extremely costly, a cost likely to be paid the following February and March when their canned rations ran short.

Another way to close the labor gap was by hiring help. But families lived on slim margins, and even a farm that did well was usually strapped for cash. So homesteaders struggled to pay hired hands. Then, too, help was hard to find when it was most needed. Farmers had no problem finding men to hire between November and March, because many local men would gladly work to pick up some extra cash. Indeed, a homesteader might look to hire himself out. But he didn't need help then. During the growing and harvesting season, however, when he really needed the extra hands, few men were looking for jobs.

Henry and Rosie Ise, on their Kansas homestead, hired a man named McAllister to help out. McAllister was a floater, new to the community, and the Ises thought him shiftless and furtive. He was greedy at the table. When he first asked for a job, sitting with the Ises at breakfast, he had refused sugar for his coffee. That was the polite thing to do because sugar was so expensive. But after he was hired Rosie caught him stealing cookies, and when he poured himself a cup of coffee, he spooned three teaspoonfuls of sugar into it.

In a coincidence of bad timing, when Rosie was lying in, Henry was called to a week's jury duty in Osborne City, the county seat. Rosie worried about McAllister doing no work with Henry's watchful eye absent. The Ises kept him on because hands were so scarce and spring work loomed. But finally Henry let him go because of his poor work habits.

In response to these constraints, the typical homesteader exploited his most readily accessible source of labor: himself. One economist labeled this "self-exploitation." He worked longer days. He worked Sunday afternoons and evenings. He worked on days when the fields were still a bit muddy. He took no days off, unless forced to do so by bad weather or injury or other circumstances. Little wonder he felt there was never enough time to finish his work—there wasn't. Homesteaders always felt there was just never enough time.

This pressure created anxiety, mental hardship, and depression, feelings that were exacerbated when crops failed and the homesteader felt himself to be a failure. Women felt the pressure of their work, too, along with the stresses of pregnancy and childbirth and, for many, loneliness, alienation, and mental fatigue. We consider women's experiences in homesteading in a later chapter. Some men dealt with their stress by quitting; others, by binge drinking, blaming others, or physically abusing their families.

Homesteaders created farms that were typically highly diversified operations. They produced field crops for sale and grew much of the family's food. They raised animals as well as plants. They tended vegetable gardens and orchards. Their work ranged from highly specialized and skilled, such as choosing the right time to plant and knowing how to manufacture clothes at home, to brute grunt labor, like cultivating dozens of acres and doing the tedious household chores of laundry and cleaning.

In 1890 most Nebraska and Kansas homesteaders cultivated between fifty and seventy-five acres. They planted about two-thirds of their fields in corn, 10–15 percent in wheat, and the rest in other small grains (oats, barley, rye, and buckwheat) and potatoes. Dakota farmers, in their less humid climate, concentrated on wheat. South Dakotans planted 60 percent of their acres in wheat; North Dakotans, 84 percent in wheat.

Farm households also devoted significant time and labor to other farm operations. Draft animals powered all the field machinery, so homesteaders gave great care to maintaining the health of their horses, oxen, and mules. Most households also had dairy cows, hogs, and chickens, and some had ducks and turkeys and sheep, all requiring time and effort. They worked in their vegetable gardens, watered and pruned the fruit trees, and butchered hogs and chickens.

For certain tasks, family labor was simply insufficient, and at such times homesteaders turned to their neighbors for help. Perhaps the biggest misconception about homesteaders is that they succeeded on their own. Purveyors of popular culture and even some scholars have elevated the image of the solitary homesteading family or individual. Homesteading success, it was alleged, rose or fell on the basis of their own labor, persistence, cleverness, and luck. The homesteaders who succeeded did so, in this view, because they worked hard, overcame adversities, and perhaps were lucky.

This image was most powerfully propelled by the bestselling books and long-running TV show, *Little House on the Prairie*. The Ingalls family appears quite self-contained and self-sufficient, except for when they were engaged in activities like barn-raising and attending school and church. Earlier writings also propagated the image of the isolated and self-reliant homesteader. Among the most influential were Elinore Pruitt Stewart's widely read letters in *The Atlantic Monthly*.

Undoubtedly some homesteaders, isolated or self-isolating, fit the stereotype. And certainly, lazy work habits or bad decisions or bum luck could sink a homesteader. But most relied heavily on their neighbors.

Homesteading typically involved a great deal of community sharing. Stringing fences, well digging, harvesting, nursing the sick or injured, filling a cistern, midwifing, retrieving strayed livestock, and even such simple tasks as picking up mail or groceries for a neighbor when in town brought rural people together. When Thor and Gjertru Birkelo homesteaded in Williams County, North Dakota, they drew their food and supplies from the town of Tioga, twenty miles away. Without cooperation these tasks became more time-consuming, harder, or even dangerous.

Easiest was sharing machinery. Most homesteaders struggled to afford a plow, disc, harrow, mower, row cultivator, binder, hay rake, reaper, straw baler, and other implements they needed. To economize, they shared. One bought some pieces of equipment, a neighbor bought others, and perhaps a third still other equipment. Men traded labor as well, sometimes simply helping each other but at other times being paid or trading labor for use of draft animals or equipment.

Such relationships were easier when those doing the sharing were brothers or cousins, belonged to the same church or ethnic group, or had served together in the war. But they could create frictions and feuds as well as friendly feelings, though they mostly went unrecorded.

Neighboring women also shared their services. They attended each other during births, nursed the sick, and bandaged the injured. They helped each other make clothes, collected berries together, and worked together when the flood of garden vegetables arrived and needed to be canned. They socialized together and organized dinners.

Mary Burden, who with husband Henry homesteaded in Saline County, Nebraska, was known to be an excellent baker of white bread. Terezie Pisar, a Czech woman living nearby, specialized in rye bread. Mrs. Pisar would occasionally cross the fields to visit Mary, and the two would exchange loaves, creating a treat for both families. Their visits offered feminine companionship as well as bread. These visits apparently satisfied both women, even though Mary spoke no Czech and Terezie, no English.

Neighbors also necessarily worked together to construct churches, open and staff country schools, and build and maintain roads. Most settlers were religious, and they saw a close connection between religious observance and divine protection from all the hazards they faced. When a traveling preacher passed through, homesteaders spread the word and held services in someone's home. Reverend Bowers sometimes preached at Henry Ise's homestead in Kansas. He could only read his Bible slowly and stumblingly, but he nonetheless had the spirit of evangelism in his heart. He preached with such power that people claimed they could hear him a mile away—two miles if the windows were open and the wind was in the right direction.

Homesteaders typically got busy organizing a local school soon after they arrived. Many were literate, and those who weren't knew the value of education, so getting children into school joined church building as a top priority. Lutherans and congregants in other Protestant sects needed to read the Bible as a crucial part of family devotions. Many Black homesteaders had been brutally denied the opportunity of learning how to read and write under slavery. They saw education as a hallmark of freedom, proof of being full and equal citizens.

Jenny Fletcher opened a school in her dugout in Nicodemus the first year the settlers arrived. Settlers in Osborne County,

**Fig. 11.** Sod schoolhouse with students and teachers, Osborne County, Kansas, 1881. Permission of the Kansas State Historical Society.

Kansas, used sod to build the walls and roof of their schoolhouse, as did others across the Great Plains.

Homesteaders also worked together to develop the roads and keep them cleared in winter. Before counties formed formal road departments and took responsibility, farmers were generally left to maintain the roads themselves. Most roads followed section lines and were just primitive trails, two ruts cut by wagon wheels defining the road. Passing traffic, if it was frequent enough, kept the prairie grasses along each side at bay. The roads could be blocked by deep snow drifts, by washouts, by mud after heavy rains, or by streams flooding their banks.

Families felt trapped when the roads were blocked. They could not get out to town to pick up their mail, call for the doctor when needed, stock up on supplies and groceries, sell their milk, eggs, and butter, or take crops to the elevator. They worried when the roads became impassable.

Collective tasks were not always done in the best humor. The principal route near Henry Ise's homestead in Osborne County, Kansas, in the 1870s was an old road in bad repair. It crossed a creek several times within the span of a mile. During heavy rains, when the creek flooded, it clogged the culverts and made the road impassable. Homesteaders north of Ise's place wanted the road moved a half-mile east to avoid the problem. But homesteaders abutting the old road wanted it to be repaired rather than moved.

The dispute got nasty. When the two sides failed to come to an agreement, they both hired lawyers in Osborne City. The court case dragged on, and the conflict split the Lutheran church—congregants from both factions refused to take communion with the other side. The quarrel aggravated other lingering irritations among neighbors, souring relations in the whole area. The court finally decided to leave the road where it was, but afterwards some families nursed grudges for years, neighbors refusing to talk to neighbors.

All these shared needs and projects forced neighbors to cooperate, sometimes unwillingly, but never did homesteaders depend on neighbors more than during the proving-up process.

The GLO required each claimant to advertise in a local newspaper the names of four potential witnesses and then actually call two of them to testify in person at the land office. Witnesses certified, under penalty of perjury, that the entryman had met all the homestead law's requirements—that he or she had constructed a dwelling and resided on the claim for five years, had taken no absences longer than six months, had plowed at least ten acres, and had made other required improvements. Friends or acquaintances who lived far away could not provide credible testimony that the claimant hadn't left his land. Only nearby neighbors were in a position to vouch for the claimant's residency.

So a homesteader's very ability to gain ownership of his claim depended on other people—his witnesses. After five or more years of hardship and toil, it all came down to this: the homesteader needed neighbors to validate his homesteading venture. If a witness lied or simply failed to show up at the land office, the homesteader might be out of luck. He might be denied his patent or at a minimum would be in for a long bureaucratic appeal process and many sleepless nights. A prejudiced witness who coveted the claimant's land for himself and was willing to testify falsely could do great damage.

Thus, successful homesteaders relied deeply on the help of neighbors for their "own" success. Rather than the solitary figures solely responsible for their own fates, homesteaders regularly needed others—to trade field labor with; to share or borrow expensive machinery and tools; to provide medical care and midwife services; to work together to construct houses, barns, and fences; to borrow draft animals when one's own animal went sore footed; to depend on for socializing and reducing the isolation and loneliness of farm life. And they needed others to witness at proving-up time. Homesteading was a highly communal activity.

The 55 percent of initial filers who succeeded, after they survived the first difficult years and made it through to proving up, then faced a decision. Most had established productive fields, built a dwelling and barn, fenced their property, gathered the stock and machinery needed to farm, and developed the requisite skills to succeed at it. The question they faced was Did they want to remain as farmers, or would they rather sell out and try town life?

Proving up meant that they now owned a valuable asset, worth more or less depending on the times and location, but even during hard times in the nineteenth century it had value.

(By contrast, some in the 1930s simply walked away from then-worthless farms.) As full owners, they could legally sell their homesteads. Proving up opened another benefit: they could pledge their land as bank collateral for a mortgage. Having been denied credit before proving up, they could now use a loan to expand their holdings, upgrade their livestock, and buy new or better implements.

Some chose to sell out. They were exhausted by the strenuous struggle to transform prairie into productive farmland. Or they decided they either were not very good at farming or they just didn't like its never-ending chores and worry. Some had suffered a change in their situations—they had been injured or worse. Josephine Denio's husband, Edgar, died shortly before she could prove up on their Custer County, Nebraska, homestead. Running a farm by herself was more than she could manage.

Some found other passions. George Washington Carver homesteaded in Ness County, Kansas, in 1886. But he was only marginally successful as a farmer, surprising for someone who, since childhood, had amazed people with his ability to nurture sick plants. His undoing was his intense curiosity, which led him to spend considerable time away from his farm. Rather than single-mindedly tending his crops, he explored geological sites, painted, and participated in literary and choral productions in town. When he got his patent, he sold out, using some of the proceeds to attend college and launch himself on his world-renowned scientific career.

Some sold out because they were in debt and could never get their heads above water, falling deeper in debt each year they farmed. Hettie and Newt Anderson were near despair after five years on their Keya Paha claim. Hettie wrote in her diary, "Homesteading is anything but what we had pictured. Though we had expected privations and hardships, we were not prepared for the trying experiences of these years of unrequited toil too great." She added, "Not one year have we succeeded in making a living off our place, though we have worked early and late and done without everything we could. We have gone deeper in debt every year, until now, only the good Lord knows whether we will get out or not."

She described being "stranded on the lonely desolate prairie of the far west (Nebraska!)." They were reduced to the last extremity of destitution. Worse still, Newt's health was broken. "He was not able to work at any price and was utterly discouraged; with no idea which way to turn for any measure of relief." They embodied the bitter rural joke about the farmer who won the Irish Sweepstakes lottery jackpot. When he was asked what he was going to do with all his new riches, he replied, "Oh, I guess I'll just farm till it's all gone."

The Andersons were saved by the arrival of eastern speculators. When others around them were simply abandoning their claims because they could find no buyers, the Andersons learned of men loaning money on homesteads that had been proved up. The homesteaders took out mortgages for a few hundred dollars on their claims, whatever the speculators would give them, and then scampered out of the area with the cash. The speculators foreclosed and thus got the land.

Newt went to town and got a mortgage for $600. "What a time of rejoicing that was!" Hettie noted in her diary. "What a God-send it proved to be to us all! How well I remember Newt's arrival home after the transaction, bringing with him a plentiful supply of things we had lacked for so long." She reflected, "After all the toil and sacrifices of these five years and disappointed hopes of having a farm, we were at least free of debt and in possession of a good team and wagon, with enough money to fit ourselves out with needed things and to take us to some favorable location." They moved to Atkinson, Nebraska, in Holt County south of Keya Paha, and eventually they migrated to California.

So there were many reasons why homesteaders sold out once they received their patents. Some scholars have misinterpreted this to allege that these claimants never intended to be "actual settlers" in the first place and were just cheaters and speculators. Perhaps some were, though as Newt and Hettie showed, they chose a very hard road, spending five long years to "cheat" their way to the prize. More had proved their fidelity by traveling that hard road, only to find their situations or dreams had changed.

Most successful filers stayed to develop flourishing farms. They were the most likely buyers of homesteads others wanted to sell. They could expand their operations beyond the original 160 or 320 acres. And the inexorable logic of American farming—grow larger to survive—stimulated rural consolidation. When hard times came, as they did in the 1870s, 1890s, 1920s, and most disastrously in the 1930s, marginal farmers or those with the least personal commitment to farming were likely to be the ones washed out. Nonetheless, the remainder who survived laid the foundation for the successful farmers of the twentieth and twenty-first centuries.

# CHAPTER FIVE

# Perils and Survival

Nineteenth-century homesteaders faced many perils. Rattlesnakes for one. Daniel Sage paid twenty dollars for a relinquishment in Custer County, Nebraska, in 1883. He broke thirty-five acres of prairie sod, during which he killed twenty-seven rattlesnakes. Homesteaders reported that rattlesnakes slithered into the warm crevices of dugouts and sod houses, and all too often people found them curled up in the bedclothes.

William and Mary Downey homesteaded in Fillmore County, Nebraska, in 1871 and built a sod house. While they were waiting for a bed they had ordered to arrive, they made a temporary bed on the dirt floor by laying a buffalo robe down and then placing their bedclothes on top. When they took it up in the morning, they discovered that during the night a rattlesnake had entered the house through a mousehole in the sod wall. It had curled up in the warm bedclothes.

Andrew Pearl, a New Yorker, and his wife Mary, from Connecticut, homesteaded in Custer County, Nebraska, in 1879. One morning their nine-year-old son, Clyde, opened the curtains behind which his two-year-old sister, Rosa, was sleeping. He was startled to see a large diamond rattler coiled beside her throat as she slept. Knowing enough not to startle the snake, he backed away and caught his mother's attention. Neither Mary nor Clyde spoke a word while she assessed the situation. The snake, alerted to their presence, crawled away, escaping into a mousehole in the wall. Rosa was not harmed, but everyone in the family was deeply shaken.

Hail was another problem. It arrived with the thunderstorms of summer and obliterated wonderfully promising wheat and corn crops. In as little as twenty minutes the hail could destroy a season's toil and a year's income. Homer and Mirinda Eggleston homesteaded in Clyde Township of Beadle County, South Dakota, in 1882. The first year Homer broke sixty acres and harvested a meager corn crop. In 1883 he raised a big crop of oats.

The next year looked to be an excellent (and profitable) year for Eggleston. His wheat crop grew bountifully on his sixty acres. In July, however, a fierce storm came through and dropped hailstones as big as goose eggs on his field. The stones laid the wheat flat on the ground and even cut up the straw. Eggleston had nothing left for all his hard work that year, and the next spring he could still see the dimples in the soil made by the hailstones.

James Nolan homesteaded in Fillmore County, Nebraska, in 1871. By his second year he had put in fifteen acres of wheat. When it was ripe and ready to cut, he traveled to Fairmont to purchase a harvester. But the night he was away, a violent rain and hailstorm beat down at his farm, and when it was over, Nolan had no need for a harvester.

Blizzards, too, struck with a sudden intensity that often caught people out in the fields or traveling away from shelter. Animals grazing in pastures froze because the drifts blocked them from returning to the barn. In Beadle County, South Dakota, Viola Peet's husband, Stewart, had gone haying on January 12, 1888, when she noticed the weather changing. "Soon, it was a smother of snow as though a great feather bed was being emptied," she said. The winds blew more violently, and the storm's intensity increased.

When Stewart failed to return, she grew worried that maybe a horse had kicked him or something. She left the baby in the house, bundled up, and went to look for him. She thought she was going toward the barn but soon realized she was lost. The whipping snow had blinded her. She bumped into a drift and fell down. She saw her tracks where she had crunched the wet snow, and following them on hands and knees, got herself to the back door. There stood Stewart, holding the baby and frantically calling her name.

Farm accidents, whether being kicked by a horse or scalding oneself with boiling water during canning, likewise threatened disaster. Ella and James Oxford homesteaded in Custer County, Nebraska, in 1874. In 1879 James made a trip to Kearney for supplies, and Ella's parents, the Hendersons, came to stay with her and the children while he was away. Grandpa Henderson went up a ravine to cut cedar trees for building. He was about to finish, but the last tree he felled unexpectedly fell on him, breaking his right arm and leg and dislocating his hip.

Grandma Henderson found him the next morning, and later that day they hauled him home on a wagon. They sent for help. Four days later Dr. Hawkins from Loup City showed up, drunk and with few actual medical skills. He amputated Henderson's arm but left the leg and hip to heal on their own. Henderson couldn't walk for a year, and afterward he walked with a crutch and a limp. He was no longer much help around the farm. Homesteading offered no sick days and was unforgiving of injuries.

As bad as rattlesnakes, hail, blizzards, farm accidents, and other dangers undoubtedly were, the three perils most feared by homesteaders were grasshoppers, prairie fires, and childbirth. All three could be deadly. (We consider childbirth in a later chapter.)

The grasshoppers—actually Rocky Mountain locusts, now extinct—arrived so unexpectedly and in such great numbers that they stunned the settlers. They had appeared in earlier decades, though apparently not in such great numbers and without much notice because settlers had not yet plowed the prairie. But in 1874 huge waves of ravenous insects flew in from the west, blackening the sky and destroying the crops. The next year, 1875, was the worst, with black masses of flying insects creating a living eclipse of the sun.

Dr. A. L. Child of the U.S. Signal Corps measured the swarm's size by clocking the insects' speed as they streamed overhead and then telegraphing to other towns for their data at the same moment. He estimated that the cloud was 1,800 miles long and at least 110 miles wide, large enough to cover the entire states of Wyoming and Colorado. Later scientists estimated the swarm to have weighed 27.5 million tons and contained some 12.5 trillion locusts. Congress called the locust "the single greatest impediment to settlement of the country between the Mississippi and the Rocky Mountains."

Farmers first noticed a few insects dropping out of the sky, like scouts of an advancing army. Soon they were more numerous, suggesting an unwelcome infestation, flitting about and emitting a low buzz. But these were still just the advance guard, because behind them came the dense black cloud stretching high in the sky and far away to the horizon. One observer said it looked like a cloud of glistening snowflakes, except the snowflakes were alive, eddying and whirling about. Then the cloud dropped its terrible burden. It hailed locusts.

They fell to the ground, making a thick, undulating carpet. They covered everything and pulsated with movement. Their buzzing crescendoed into a roar. Millions or billions of them coated the ground and everything else, their greedy jaws constantly moving and testing everything they touched. They

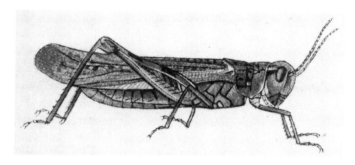

**Fig. 12.** Rocky Mountain locust (*Melanoplus spretus*), now extinct. Illustration via Wikimedia Commons.

consumed crops, leaving only short stalks here and there, and when they departed, the fields were as bare as after fall tilling. They devastated gardens.

Others of this voracious horde attacked leather harnesses, wooden shovel handles, yokes, ropes, clothing, haystacks, corn cribs, almost everything. They drowned on the surface of ponds, wells, cisterns, and pails of water, their floating carcasses forming a thick brownish-green scum. They piled up, the dead and dying forming throbbing heaps of greenish bodies. Wherever people walked, they crunched live locusts underfoot.

The homesteaders tried everything to stop them, all to no avail. When they went into the fields to try to squish them or scare them away, the hungry locusts attacked their clothes. When they started fires or blasted shotguns or sprayed poison, their efforts were so puny compared to the mass of insects that they had no effect. They constructed weird-looking "harvesters" to collect and burn the bodies, but these efforts, too, were tiny compared to the mass of their antagonists. Most of the stunned humans simply prayed for divine relief because all human efforts seemed useless.

Robert Anderson, a freedman, homesteaded in Butler County, Nebraska, in 1870. He found the following decade to be filled with heartbreak. From 1874 to 1877 the terrible armies of locusts came, and insects rained down on his farm. The insatiable creatures ate up everything he had planted. Four years of drought followed the locusts, and the sun burned up his fields. "A great many times during my years on that homestead, it was a case of jackrabbit or no breakfast. It wasn't so bad in the summer time, but in the winter it was pretty hard to live at all." He proved up, and the GLO issued him a patent on April 1, 1875. But he was unable to make the land support him, and in 1881 he simply walked away. He lost the land, his patent a bitter April Fools' joke.

James Nolan, on his Fillmore County homestead, had his wheat already harvested when the grasshoppers came, but in about an hour they ate up all his corn and the vegetable garden his wife, Eliza, had planted. The locusts left only the stumps of cabbages. Eliza's brother, George Nugent, also a Fillmore County homesteader, had a small tobacco patch that the locusts completely devoured, leaving the field picked clean. Nugent claimed that if they had only waited, he would have gotten them a gross of pipes so they could have enjoyed a good smoke.

Henry and Rosie Ise were at a funeral when they first noticed a flurry of locusts. They grew more worried as they hurried back to their homestead in Osborne County, Kansas. Henry went to inspect the garden and discovered insects covering the onion, cabbage, and tomato plants and on the weeds along the edge of the garden. He checked the cornfield and returned to Rosie, horrified. "They're eating the garden and the corn!" he told her. Every time they opened the door, locusts flew in. The pests chewed holes in the curtains and in the clothes hanging on the wall and landed in the kettles and milk pans.

Rosie and Henry decided to try to cut what corn plants remained and save it for cattle fodder. They marched out to the field, covered up in bonnets and hats, long sleeves, and gloves and set to work. Henry cut what remained of the stalks, and Rosie piled them into shocks. The insects attacked the shocks but could only eat the outsides and couldn't get at the insides. The couple worked until midnight, producing two long rows of shocks, and planned to resume the next morning. But when they woke up, they could see that the locusts had left nothing further to save.

The swarm stayed on the Ises' farm for nearly a week. The wind blew from the southeast, and the Ises sensed that the fluttering bugs were unwilling to struggle against it. Finally, the wind turned around to blow from the west, and the throbbing mass flew off, almost as quickly as it had arrived.

The catastrophe left behind was not over, however. When Henry went to draw water from the well, the pail was filled with insects. He worked patiently to rid the well water of them, but when he went back the next morning, it was again full of locusts. They clung to the walls of the deep hole, unable to fly out, and as they got weaker, they fell into the water. The well was the Ises' only source of water, so they drank from it despite how much the water stank. Even when Rosie used it to make rye coffee, attempting to disguise its foul taste, they could still taste grasshopper. The well only cleared up weeks later.

The locusts showed the brute force of nature. There was nothing humans could do, no preventative or remedial acts that could stop them. There were no best practices. The usual prescriptions for combating drought or blizzards or rattlesnakes—"work harder, be more careful, be patient"—seemed useless in the face of such an implacable and uncountable foe. Understandable that so many homesteaders turned to prayer.

Homesteaders' longer-run anxiety about the locusts was, Will they come every year? They came sparingly in 1874, then arrived in massive numbers in 1875, and returned again in diminished force in 1877. Then they disappeared for the next fifteen years. There were smaller plagues, still locally devastating, in the 1890s. Then they vanished entirely; the last sighting of a live specimen was recorded in 1902.

The locusts' disappearance was as mysterious as their arrival had been. Scientists and others have suggested many theories for the cause of their extinction. Biologist Jeffrey Lockwood proposed the leading explanation, which is that the Rocky Mountain locust, like the Monarch butterfly, had a highly specific breeding ground. It only bred in the mountain valleys of Montana and Wyoming. As settlers moved into these valleys, they cut down the trees and plowed the earth, disrupting the locusts' reproductive sequence and triggering their extinction.

Prairie fires scared homesteaders the most. Joseph Vanvalin moved with his wife to Nuckolls County, Nebraska, in 1873. Mrs. Vanvalin claimed, "What we considered the greatest thing with which we had to contend was the prairie fires."

Fires could run unchecked over immense areas—one in Kansas in 1884 damaged parts of seven western counties. Whether started by lightning strikes or careless humans, fires roared through the dry bluestem at terrifying speed. The head fire, whipped along by howling prairie winds, produced the most calamitous inferno of intense heat. The side fires along its edges lingered, as though waiting for a wind shift to make them the head fires. Unlike forest fires, prairie fires quickly burned all their fuel and either swept on or flickered out.

On April 8, 1887, in Beadle County, South Dakota, two women in their early twenties, Annie Murreen and Kate Maloney, saw a head fire coming directly toward them. They raced through the tall grass trying to outrun it and reach the safety of an island of plowed ground. But the fire was faster than the women could run. Annie's parents, who were several miles away, saw the smoke and frantically drove their wagon to rescue the women. Annie died lying in the wagon on the trip home. Kate, a teacher, lingered for ten days in horrible pain and then died.

One lazy summer day in 1907 my father, Roy Edwards, nine years old, was doing his chore of driving the family cows to the creek to water them and then heading them back home. He was accompanied by his five-year-old brother, Carroll. As the boys drove the cows toward the homestead, they started playing with matches. Young boys always like playing with fire, but Roy and Carroll must have found it especially naughty and thus fun to play with fire on the prairie. They lit a small fire and stomped it out. They lit a second one and stomped it out. They lit a third, but before they could stomp it out, it spread into the surrounding grasses and got away.

The boys were terrified. They knew if anyone learned they had started a prairie fire they'd be in serious trouble. They never found out how far it burned. They swore to each other never tell anyone about it. Roy kept his secret until he was in his sixties when he unexpectedly told his granddaughter. Even as he revealed his secret a half-century later, he shook with emotion, visibly distressed at the shameful memory. Even little boys knew prairie fires were not to be played with.

It was often the sight or smell of smoke that first alerted people to a fire. Then, as the flames raced toward houses, barns, livestock, and everything they owned, they heard its appalling roar. No living thing could survive a grass fire's intense (if brief) heat except seeds and roots in the earth. Fires sucked the oxygen out of the air, and the smoke smothered people gasping for breath. The wind could change directions and drive the fire anywhere. Sometimes when it turned suddenly it surprised people who thought they were safe, who then saw their homes and animals burned up. Other times it veered off, saving people who were sure the fire was going to get them.

Ella and James Oxford homesteaded on the north edge of Custer County, Nebraska. One day in 1878 they saw a fire sweeping toward them from the northwest. Ella placed some prized possessions in a bedsheet and gathered up the children as they stood in the yard watching the flames approach. James ran to the creek, which lay between them and the fire. He walked back and forth in the stream and threw water on the far bank. The flames approached within a quarter mile, but then the wind changed, and they were saved.

Many others were not so lucky. Nicodemus, Kansas, homesteaders had come from Kentucky, where prairie fires were unknown. In 1878 a fire killed Henry Blackman and Peter Jackson and burned up some of the community's precious food supplies.

Near Merna, in Custer County, Nebraska, on April 17, 1899, homesteader John Koch was fighting a furious fire, labelled the West Table fire. He worked frantically alongside his three grown sons. His second wife and their small children were at the house farther up the canyon, and Koch told his boys he was going to check on them. A heavy man, he made it only halfway home before the fire caught up with him, and he died.

Thomas Morrissey homesteaded nearby and tried desperately to get his horses out of the barn, which had a straw roof. But the fire was quicker, and when the flames consumed the barn it killed Morrissey too. Virtually every rural neighborhood had memories of someone killed in a prairie fire.

Walter Tucker, out from Missouri, homesteaded in Lincoln County, Nebraska. In April 1907 he was working on his brother's farm five miles from home. His daughter was hauling corn from the brother's farm to their home with a team and wagon. She got halfway with her load when she began to smell smoke coming from the northwest. Suddenly a friend, Charles Kidwell, came galloping up and tied his horse to the team. He jumped up onto the wagon seat.

"There's a prairie fire right behind us, hang on, we have got to hurry or it will catch us."

He lashed the team. Corn flew out of the wagon and scattered across the prairie. The wind switched to the east, pushing the head fire away from the Tucker place, but the side fire kept advancing closer. Kidwell herded the range cows in from one pasture and gathered the milk cows from another.

They saved Tucker's farm, but neighbors suffered terribly. The fire burned to the ground all the buildings of the Yonker family, and it killed all their livestock, cows in the feed lot, horses in the barn, pigs in their pens. J. M. Werley and his two older sons left home to fight the fire. His wife and two younger sons stayed home. They were kept busy by the streams of jackrabbits running from the fire. The rabbits' fur was on fire. Mrs. Werley and her boys clubbed them before they could set fire to the haystacks and barn.

The Tuckers' relative, Eddie Kain, was killed by the fire when his horse went down. Eddie was set afire, his clothes burned off except for his boots. He walked a mile and a half home, but he lived only a few hours. His stock perished with him as well. He left a widow and two small children.

Even if the humans escaped, the losses could be devastating. James Henry Reeder—the GLO reversed his first two names on his patent—also homesteaded in the Myrna area of Custer County. Drought in the early 1890s browned the grasses, creating a perfect setting for fire. The dry conditions also produced a meager hay crop, and Reeder, like his West Table neighbors,

**Fig. 13.** Prairie fire, menace to the homesteaders. Drawing by Adam Edwards Mayhew.

had cut and piled up as much hay as there was. When the flames came through, his haystacks and even the haybarn caught fire.

Reeder could see through the lighter haze of the prairie fire the darker, denser smoke that marked the destruction of his summer's work. The conflagration had consumed all the grass in the pasture, and now the hay was gone too. Reeder and his panicked cattle faced a bleak winter.

Unlike locusts, against which nothing seemed to help, homesteaders worked tirelessly to protect themselves from prairie fires. They had three tools: fireguards, backfires, and direct combat. These methods could be effective, though they were by no means infallible.

Homesteaders plowed wide swathes of ground around their homesteads to create firebreaks. The theory was that if the fire reached bare ground, and the bare ground was wide enough, the fire would have no fuel to advance. The swathe would act just like a river or stream, or sometimes even a railroad cut, to stop it. First, they plowed several furrows, creating a break a rod or two wide around the house and barn as an inner defense. Then they created a longer loop to enclose the garden, orchard, and small pasture as well. Some families burned off the vegetation between the breaks.

But with many urgent tasks around the homestead demanding attention, men found plowing a firebreak was easy to put off. All too often, smoke from an approaching fire induced hurried plowing that should have been done months before. One windy Saturday morning in early October 1907, George and Cara Perry, homesteaders in Sheridan County, Nebraska, were digging potatoes with their son Dallas. George had just finished turning over the rows, and he unhooked the tug on the team's singletrees. Cara saw the fire first.

"George! Look!"

George saw the fire and ran for the plow. He rehooked the tugs and set off with the team trotting toward the north fence gate. Just beyond lay an old fireguard that was due for its annual fall plowing, but George hadn't gotten to it yet. George hurriedly plowed a few furrows as the head fire roared closer. Their neighbors, including the Clausens, showed up to help.

Just beyond the fire break was a wide sand draw. The firefighters managed to use the draw to turn the fire north toward a railroad cut. By the time fire reached George's new plowing, it was a side fire. They beat the flames out with wet gunnysacks.

But just as the exhausted men were about to go home, sparks jumped the draw and lit a big fire on its east side. It headed southeast, threatening the neighboring Clausen homestead. There was no fire guard on that side of the draw, and the fire advanced rapidly. The men raced across the blackened grass in the spring wagon to check on the homestead shack. They feared the fire had burned it down and killed the several family members inside. They were relieved to see the shack still standing. It had a tiny fringe of unburned edging around all four walls. Other settlers had arrived to fight the fire, and they had been able to "herd" it to death against a plowed field.

H. A. Johnson was returning home after battling but not containing part of the big West Table fire. He came upon the Shaw family, recent homesteaders who had just come out from Missouri. They knew nothing of prairie fires, but they could see it would burn their frame house if it reached that far. They were carrying their household goods and children to a cellar, which would likely have been a suffocating death trap if the fire had raced over the top of them. Johnson told them to hitch their team to a plow, and he plowed a wide fire guard for them. When he returned later, Mrs. Shaw came to the door, tears running down her cheeks. She told him, "Mr. Johnson, you kept us from burning up."

Homesteaders also regularly fought fire with backfires. They burned a space under controlled circumstances so that when the prairie fire came through, they had already burned its fuel and it would flicker out. Marion and Martha Ann Hays, Custer County, Nebraska, homesteaders in 1883, were returning from Kearney with their children and a load of supplies. They could see an approaching prairie fire. They jumped out of the wagon and immediately began to burn the area around them. By the time the prairie fire reached them, they had burned a large enough area that they were quite safe as the prairie fire swept by.

Richard and Elizabeth Eubank, who homesteaded in Morrill County, Nebraska, in 1879, combined these methods. He plowed a firebreak near the house, then plowed another one much farther out, and then burned the whole area between the two. Even so, a prairie fire driven by extreme winds jumped the first fire guard. Richard was away, but Elizabeth saw the fire coming and ran to the barn to untie their two bronco ponies before the fire burned them up. The ponies snorted and lunged and were gone. One pony was recaptured six weeks later; the other was never seen again.

But backfires were dangerous because they could easily get out of control and cause a wider prairie fire. In Beadle County, South Dakota, a homesteader named Hull was reported to have been burning off a patch of weeds when the fire got away from him. His neighbors, the Chase family, lost their barns, horses, machinery—everything. At a time when farmers' insurance was virtually unknown, such losses were shattering.

The last line of defense was to attack the fire directly. When flames came near, neighbors quickly mobilized to stamp them out by brute force. Someone would hitch a team to a spring wagon, load up barrels or milk cans with water, and head to the fire line. The wagon followed along the line so firefighters could wet their gunny sacks over and over as needed. Men, and often women as well, and the older children would wet their sacks, tarps, brooms, and coats—anything that could be used to smother the flames. Working along the head fire was especially dangerous, more so for women who risked setting the hems of their skirts on fire.

Beating down the flames of side fires was easier but not easy. Men would sometimes hook drooping chains between two horses and then ride along the fire line, one horse on each side, to knock out the fire.

The struggle ended when they put out the fire, or more likely, when the wind shifted or it rained or some other factor intervened to stop it.

Despite the many perils they faced, most homesteaders not only survived but thrived. Some, of course, were crushed and abandoned the region, sunk under the financial or psychic weight of failed crops, dead children or spouses, disabling accidents, or any of a dozen other setbacks that flattened their dreams. They made up the 45 percent who "failed."

But others held on, struggling through the hard years and catastrophes to build thriving farms. They worked patiently, year by year, to extend their fields, construct barns and granaries, accumulate farm implements, nurture gardens and fruit trees, raise livestock and chickens, and transform their raw homesteads into productive farms. The Ises, Svendsbyes, Trews, Haneys, Fletchers, and others overcame the perils they faced, and by their own grit and often the generous and timely help of neighbors, succeeded.

The Greatest Generation was said to have been formed by the severe challenges it faced in the Great Depression and the Second World War. They came through those fires, it is said, tempered and hardened and shaped into individuals who were modest, frugal, resolute, and highly motivated. So equipped, they went on to make great achievements. So too, perhaps, the homesteading generation was formed by having had to overcome its great obstacles and perils, which gave them the strength and quiet self-confidence to achieve great things.

# CHAPTER SIX

# Black Homesteaders

Black people homesteaded in all the Great Plains states. While many fewer in number than whites, they filed claims during the entire homesteading period. Mathew Pitman, the first Black man to file for a homestead in Nebraska, entered his initial claim for Lancaster County land in June 1869. William E. Royster homesteaded in Yellowstone County, Montana, on the western edge of the Great Plains. He earned his patent in 1944.

Black migrants to the Great Plains were mostly formerly enslaved people or their descendants. Some had fled from bondage before the Civil War, some escaped to the advancing Union armies, and others were freed by the Thirteenth Amendment.

Black people rejoiced at the promises of Reconstruction. They especially looked forward to the prospect of being given "forty acres and a mule" and to owning the Southern fields they had worked for so long.

But Southern whites responded to Blacks' new freedom with ferocious violence. Whites used intimidation and murder to deny Black people land. In the corrupt Compromise of 1877 Republican presidential candidate Rutherford B. Hayes agreed to end Reconstruction and withdraw federal troops from the South in return for gaining the electoral votes he needed to win the presidency. Black people's dreams of building new lives on their own farms in the South lay shattered.

Some Black people began to look westward for the opportunity to own land. Black Americans at the end of the nineteenth century, observes historian Quintard Taylor, "had come to believe that the only way they could have true freedom was to have ownership over a piece of land." They became interested in the government's offer of homesteads. Most Black homesteaders, about 70 percent of them, migrated and homesteaded as part of organized communities or what they called "colonies." They identified with the Jews, another people who had been held in bondage for generations past and then made their exodus to freedom in the Promised Land.

Three hundred eight Black people launched the first and most enduring colony when they boarded a train in September 1877 in Lexington, Kentucky. They left the lush and forested bluegrass country on a journey they hoped would bring them to a new Promised Land. Another large group from Kentucky joined them the following spring. Their Canaan was called Kansas, and the community they founded was named Nicodemus.

Two of the migrants were Zachary Taylor (Z. T.) Fletcher and his wife Frances (Jenny) Fletcher. Z. T. wrote, "I being raised a slave, I have no Record of my age. My first Master was a Batchler and he Died when I was a Baby and willed all of his Slaves to his Sister Mary who had married a Man by the name of Antny Robb and She died in a few years and we was all Diveed out with her children."

Fletcher was like most who came to Nicodemus and indeed many Black people who came to the Great Plains. He carried deep memories of being enslaved and of the bitterly broken hopes of Reconstruction. But rather than being defeated and dispirited, Z. T. and Jenny arrived brimming with entrepreneurial energy, ambition, hope, and grit.

They arrived in the fall of 1877. Z. T. soon went off to work in Topeka to raise badly needed cash, while Jenny stayed to endure the first terrible winter and near famine in their dugout. With spring, however, their energies began to bear fruit. Z. T. filed on a homestead claim (though he never proved it up) and later filed a timber culture claim for which he did receive patent. Jenny ran a school in their dugout, attended by fifteen to forty-five students at different times. Z. T. opened a general store—"generally out of everything store" as his customers sometimes grumbled—and Jenny served as postmaster for the community, operating out of Z. T.'s store.

Elvira Williams came with her husband, Thorton, and seven small children in the spring of 1878. They had very few household goods and little money. They had always lived in the woods in Kentucky, and when she saw their homestead, she was disappointed and discouraged. "It was such an unusual place. I wondered if we could live there. There was nothing to arrest the sight and my eyes ached from looking so far and seeing nothing." After two days on the homestead, she was so dejected she broke down crying. "I wanted to stop crying but just couldn't."

Thorton said to her, "Now, Vira, don't take on so, there's no sense in that, we have got to try to stay here. We can't move away, and if we work as hard here as we did in Kentucky, we ought to be able to make a living for the children and besides we will have a home of our own, same as the rich people in Kentucky had."

They stayed and worked hard. That first summer Thorton spaded up a big garden, and they planted beans, squash, and a few rows of corn. Thorton continued to enlarge the garden each year, and Elvira and the children cared for it when he was away at work. "In a few seasons [Thorton] had a field to farm instead of a garden," Vira recalled.

Gradually they became accustomed to this weird environment. Elvira remembered how, when her boys grew old enough to leave home and work, each of them sent money home. That allowed Thorton to stay home, and they could carry on. "I got used to the prairie life after awhile and became satisfied. The little sod house was home. I was happy."

This land surely tested the newcomers' deep belief that owning land would bring them freedom. They brought with them memories of what they had experienced back "home." They wanted to build a community beyond the close scrutiny of white authority and one that was free of the South's pervasive white violence. They believed in their bones that owning land was the surest path to their larger goal. But could they succeed in such a harsh and unwelcoming place?

The town of Nicodemus grew quickly in the 1880s, becoming a vital center for business and even featuring a bank. But after 1888 it declined precipitously when railroads passed it by and Graham County voters chose another town to be their county seat.

Still, the Black homesteader population in the countryside persevered. The Nicodemus colonists earned 114 homestead patents by 1899, making them owners of 18,115 acres. Some also leased or purchased additional land. Nicodemus Township (including the town) peaked at 501 residents in 1907, and it still had 207 Black residents as late as 1940.

Black migrants established other homesteader communities as well. The most important were DeWitty, Nebraska; Dearfield, Colorado; Sully County, South Dakota; Empire, Wyoming; and Blackdom, New Mexico. And Black homesteaders also settled in many smaller clusters in Kansas, Oklahoma, and elsewhere.

For Black migrants, owning land was both a means to improving their families' material lives and something much more: they wanted to own land to be free. Owning land was the key. Jeannettee Parton, a descendant of Sully County Black homesteaders, remembered, "My family sacrificed everything for

**Fig. 14.** William Meehan, son of DeWitty, Nebraska, homesteaders and a talented young poet, circa 1916. Courtesy of Catherine Meehan Blount.

their land. Success was born and found in the land. Everything we had came from the land." Forrest Stith, writing about his grandparents at DeWitty, simply noted, "Ownership of land was a true symbol of freedom to the former slaves and their offspring."

Wayne Brown, an Omaha lawyer and sixth-generation descendant of DeWitty, said his ancestors desired the opportunity to own some land. As he put it, "There's something special that goes to the heart of every African American, it's that promise of 40 acres and a mule and having the opportunity to be an owner in America. . . . Owning a piece of America as the descendants of former slaves, that is the highest form of freedom, to own property in America. It's still the highest form of freedom."

The Black homesteader communities shared a powerful commitment to education. Many of the migrants were illiterate, because slaveowners made it illegal to teach enslaved people how to read and write. Nicodemus residents were reminded of this traumatic past whenever they glimpsed the face of Rev. Simon Roundtree, leader of the first group of Lexington migrants. As a young boy, Roundtree was secretly being taught to read by the son of his owner. However, the owner discovered them. As punishment, he branded Roundtree on the cheek. Roundtree carried the scar, a visible reminder of how precious education was, the rest of his long life.

All Black homesteaders carried as shared memory the terrible ordeal of slavery, even those who had not themselves been enslaved. Later migrants learned of slavery's horrors from parents, aunts and uncles, and grandparents. The homesteaders' ambitions, anxieties, and dreams were necessarily shaped by that past. And they saw being educated as an essential aspect of being free and fully equal citizens. They sacrificed and invested to ensure that their descendants would never have to sign official documents with an *X*, as some of them did.

As soon as they established their communities, Black homesteaders set about arranging for the education of their children and grandchildren. Jenny Fletcher opened her school in the first year after arrival in Nicodemus. Homesteaders at DeWitty established school districts 108, 110, 113, and 164 in their first couple of years. Formalizing districts created taxing authorities and a framework that allowed parents to construct and manage the one-room schoolhouses. At Empire, the community leader, Rev. Russel Taylor, was also the schoolmaster, and he worked energetically to get a schoolhouse built and obtain resources from an unaccommodating county school board.

The cost of the homesteaders' commitment to education was not small. They poured their energies, time, emotions, talents, and money—cash that struggling farmers always found so hard to come by—into the schools. They constructed school buildings, paid teachers (many who came from their own communities), purchased books, lobbied county school boards for funds, served on local school boards, ordered library books, and stood over children's homework in the evenings. The parents knew how far their own toil and struggle had taken them, and they expected even greater achievements from their children.

Despite the difficulties and vicissitudes of Great Plains farming, Black homesteaders created communities that were centers of communal identity, recreation, culture, joy, pride, and achievement. For those fleeing the oppression and violence of the South, they found, in the words of Nicodemus descendant Angela Bates, "a place where they could experience real freedom."

Nicodemus residents exulted in that freedom to create a lively community life for themselves. They organized African Methodist Episcopal (AME) and Baptist churches. The churches became centers of civic, as well as religious, activities. Residents formed the Nicodemus Literary Society, the Grand Benevolent

Society, the Daughters of Zion, the Nicodemus Emigration Society, the Cornet Band, and other cultural and civic betterment groups. To foster business, they formed the Nicodemus Joint Stock Company and the Nicodemus Land Company. They put on dances in a grove outside of town. They created two newspapers, the *Nicodemus Enterprise* and the *Western Cyclone*.

They organized big community celebrations on the Fourth of July and Emancipation Day. They celebrated Emancipation Day around August 1 to honor the date in 1834 when the British Empire made slavery illegal. Organizers filled both days with music, races, children's games, ice cream, baseball, boxing matches, food stalls, dancing, and other diversions. Speakers always provided the capstone. They recounted in magnetic oratory the trials of the race's past and the glorious prospects facing residents in the future.

DeWitty residents likewise created rich religious and civic lives for themselves. Much of DeWitty's social life revolved around the church. Residents affiliated with various denominations, but most, regardless of affiliation, supported the local St. James AME Church. In 1910 community members held a fundraiser to convert an old sod schoolhouse into their house of worship. Everyone pitched in, even those who could not donate money. Residents made the furniture and acquired a pump organ and stoves; the Cherry County, Nebraska, judge donated a large Bible.

DeWitty residents created social organizations and shared events and pastimes to amuse themselves and draw the community together. Robert Hannahs, a local barber, annually hosted a big community picnic on the first Sunday of August. Residents contributed food and games, music, speeches, and sometimes organized a rodeo. The community always celebrated the Fourth of July, another big occasion for sharing food, fun, and games, with the nearby white town of Brownlee.

**Fig. 15.** The Robert Hannahs family, DeWitty, Nebraska, circa 1915.
Permission of History Nebraska.

DeWitty residents were passionate about baseball, and their team, the Sluggers, played teams from Brownlee, Thedford, Seneca, and elsewhere. The Sluggers were very good, well known throughout the region for suffering few losses between 1910 and 1920. Musicians in the community formed bands that played at dances and weddings, often touring throughout western Nebraska.

Some Black migrants homesteaded by themselves, unaffiliated with any Black community. One was Henry Burden, who filed his claim in Saline County, Nebraska. Burden saved his army bonus and Atwood House wages to launch his real ambition: to own land.

On a bright spring day in early April 1870, he traveled twenty-five miles southwest of Lincoln to Crete, a recently settled village of about a thousand people. He then drove his team and wagon another ten miles over prairie trails, really just two ruts in the grass, to Pleasant Hill, an even newer settlement of about a hundred people. He still had another two or three miles farther south to go. He had no markers to guide him through the raw prairie except perhaps a game trail.

Then he stopped. He started to build his future in a place with few other people around and no structure to shield him from the summer sun or the coming winter cold. He staked out an eighty-acre homestead and filed his claim on April 8, 1870.

As a Black man Burden was unique in Saline County. Not rare—unique. The 1870 census reported Saline contained 3,106 people, with none of them Black (Burden likely arrived after the count was taken). Surrounded by a sea of grass and with white people as his only neighbors—with no house on the property yet, with the tough prairie sod to break before he could even begin to farm—he must have felt very, very alone. But remembering how far he had come—his escape from slavery in Petersburg, working and being frugal and saving his money in the years afterward—he also must have been elated. He was standing on ground he would soon own. He was going, quite literally, from being owned to owning.

Burden built a fourteen-by-sixteen-foot house of pine lumber. He constructed an eight-by-twenty-foot frame granary and a stable. He dug a well. He cultivated thirty acres, likely planted with corn. He planted twenty-five apple trees and a number of shade trees.

Burden worked hard and refused to be defeated by setbacks. The 1870s were especially brutal. Burden's farm was threatened by a devastating tornado that hit Saline County in May 1872, and then he barely escaped damage from a calamitous prairie fire on October 14, 1873. His first wife, Eliza Hill, died in childbirth in 1873, along with his stillborn son. Heavy rains on July 25, 1875, produced unprecedented flooding throughout Saline. Floodwater filled Turkey Creek just west of Pleasant Hill from "hill to hill." All of Saline County was disastrously attacked by locusts in 1874 and 1876. Many farmers saw their crops destroyed and gave up, moving off the land. Burden stayed.

Burden was helped through these hard times by George Hastings, a white man who loaned him money. Hastings was a partner in the Pleasant Hill law firm of McGinty and Hastings, and he advanced Burden some funds, how much is unknown. The two men wrote up conditions for this aid in the form of a loan contract, perhaps to spare embarrassment on both sides. But given the county's dire circumstances, and especially Burden's poverty, Hastings undoubtedly considered it more as neighborly charity than a financial investment. In any event, it helped Henry get through the crisis.

Burden married Mary Barbour in 1878. Mary was born into slavery, like Henry, in Alabama, probably in 1847. They had eight children, the first they named George Hastings Burden. Henry and Mary remained married until she died in 1895.

Years later Burden remembered that old "loan" he had received from George Hastings that had helped him survive the 1870s. When he became more successful, Henry had the means to make good on the loan. He traveled to Crete to look up Hastings, by then a retired judge. Hastings expressed great surprise and said he was not expecting repayment. But Burden insisted. They found the old loan document, and Burden repaid the judge, officially clearing his "debt."

Henry remained on his homestead until his death in 1913. By then he had become a pillar of the community, a longtime treasurer on the board of trustees of his (mostly white) church and the sole Black member of the F. J. Coates Post of the Grand Army of the Republic.

The Saline community responded to Henry's death with a tremendous outpouring of respect and sympathy. His funeral on October 13 attracted a big crowd of mourners. All the local papers—the *Crete News*, the *Friend Telegraph* (Friend, Nebraska), the *Crete Democrat*, the *Dorchester Star*, the *DeWitt Times Union*, and more—reported his death, in most cases as a major news story on the front page as well as in more stylized obituaries. The *Wilber Republican* extolled him, saying Henry Burden was "kind, polite and obliging, almost to a fault, honest and true as the needle to the pole, and his unswerving honesty, his integrity, his abhorrence of all that was mean, dishonest and vicious gained for him the reputation which extended far beyond the boundaries of Saline county."

Robert Anderson was another Black man who homesteaded by himself, unaffiliated with a colony. He was born into slavery in Kentucky in 1843. As a young child he witnessed his mother being sold away. He never saw her again. He endured a harsh adolescence, which included being beaten by his owner's wife. Anderson escaped to the Union Army and joined up during the war. He later served as a buffalo soldier in the West.

He developed a fierce desire to own land. He worked as a farm laborer, saved his wages and army pay, and bought some land in Iowa. However, a land agent cheated him, and his land was worthless, leaving him broke. He worked for more years and again saved his money. He homesteaded in Butler and Lancaster counties in eastern Nebraska in the 1870s. But he lost those claims to locusts and drought. He was broke again. He worked as a laborer for three more years, again carefully saving his money.

He moved to western Nebraska, to Box Butte County, in 1884, to start over yet again. Box Butte is much more arid than his previous claims in Butler and Lancaster counties had been. Having exhausted his right to claim a homestead, he instead filed a timber culture claim and a few years later purchased a relinquishment.

Buying a claim before it was proved up was illegal because the claimant didn't yet own the land. An abandoned (relinquished) claim reverted to the GLO and went back into the government's pool of available land. So to get around this restriction, the seller and buyer of a relinquishment agreed to go to the land office together. When the seller officially relinquished his claim, the buyer stood as the next person in line, ready to claim it. "Buying a relinquishment" meant agreeing to this arrangement. Because the seller was not technically selling the land, the GLO paid little attention to relinquishments. The buyer still had to fulfill all the GLO's homesteading requirements, including residency, building a dwelling, and so on.

Anderson marshalled everything he had learned from his unsuccessful ventures in Iowa and eastern Nebraska. This time he succeeded. He built a two-room sod house. He raised a small amount of wheat, had a good garden that he carefully watered from his well, and stocked his table with rabbits and grouse. To save money, he did almost every task on the ranch himself. He added a few head of horses and a cow. He built frame additions to enlarge his sod home and attached a barn. He said, "I learned that the soil would raise anything if properly cared for." He was extremely frugal, continuing a lifelong habit.

By then well-tutored in the cruel Great Plains climate, Anderson survived the lean years of the 1890s drought. In fact, he thrived. He watched as the drought, just like the one in the 1870s that had driven him off his Butler County homestead, drove his neighbors off their Box Butte land. Confident that rainfall would return, he purchased their failed farms. By 1896 Anderson owned 480 acres, some of which he plowed to raise wheat and oats. He continued purchasing his neighbors' land, increasing his holdings to 1,280 acres in 1902 and to 2,080 acres by 1918. He had become a prosperous, well-established landowner—as he titled his memoir, he had gone "From Slavery to Affluence."

Oscar Micheaux was a Black homesteader who suffered too much success. Micheaux's parents had been enslaved, and when freed they moved across the Ohio River to southern Illinois, where Oscar grew up. He was the fifth child of thirteen, and the children, especially boys, were expected to help out with the interminable farm chores. Oscar later admitted that his brothers did most of the field work, as he found it too cold to work in the winter and too warm in the summer. He did better at selling the family goods at the local market, where he began cultivating an easy charm that won customers, white as well as Black.

Micheaux left home in 1900 when he was sixteen. That year only 6 percent of seventeen-year-olds of all races graduated high school, and Oscar was not among them. He worked his way north. At eighteen he talked his way into a job as a Pullman railcar porter, one of the elite positions open to Black men at the time. He worked as a porter for several years.

During his long trips across country, from Seattle or San Francisco to Philadelphia or Washington, he marveled at the fertile fields. He developed a yearning to own land. He especially liked what he saw riding the rails between Chicago and Denver. The farmer's son who had shirked working in the fields and fled his hometown now dreamed of owning his own farm.

In 1904 Micheaux learned that President Theodore Roosevelt had declared part of the Rosebud Reservation in South Dakota open for homesteading. To prevent repeating the chaos of the Oklahoma land runs, the GLO organized a lottery to handle the expected crush of land seekers to determine who could claim the 2,400 available homesteads. It held the drawing on July 28, 1904. When Micheaux saw his ticket was number 6,504, he was distraught. He realized his chance of getting a claim was hopeless.

Micheaux returned to portering. But in October he traveled back to South Dakota, thinking that some of the lottery winners would not really want to farm and might be willing to relinquish their claims for cash. He was right, and he bought his first relinquishment in Gregory County, South Dakota.

He quit his portering job and started farming in earnest in 1905. With the help of a sod mason, he built a low sod house, fourteen by sixteen feet, with a hipped roof. He dug a well, added a fourteen-by-sixteen-foot granary, a barn, and a shed. After a faltering start with two balky mules, he began breaking the prairie for fields.

He carefully rotated his crops, probably to learn what would grow well and also to maintain soil quality and respond to fluctuating crop prices. On the first tract of prairie he broke he planted corn (1905), wheat (1906), flax (1907), oats (1908), and corn (1909). He faced many hardships—horses straying, drought, grasshoppers, hail, stripe rust on the wheat, and deep snow drifts that could kill livestock. He worried about crop prices. And like everyone, he feared prairie fire. One fire destroyed much of the nearby town of Dallas and appeared ready to consume Oscar's fields when, at the last moment, the wind shifted direction and he averted disaster.

He also accumulated more land. Expanding on his initial 160-acre claim, in 1906 he bought another relinquishment some miles away, north of the town of Gregory. He invited his maternal grandmother, Louisa Goff, and his sister, Olivia Micheaux, to file claims as soon as the government opened up more land in nearby Tripp County. He paid $1,200 for a relinquishment for Orlean McCracken, his future bride.

He and his female relatives now owned eight hundred acres, scattered across five locations in two counties, for him to farm. He found it exhausting. On one occasion he was away hauling coal to a Tripp County farm to fuel a steam tractor that he had contracted to break sod. While he was absent from home, his wife, Orlean, had given birth to a stillborn son. She never forgave him for being away and leaving her alone. They soon divorced, not amicably.

After ten years of successful farming, during which his fields expanded but so did the mortgages that financed his land purchases, Micheaux had had enough. He had achieved "success"—his acreage and his personal wealth had greatly increased—but he was exhausted. The stress of managing five separate farms had run him ragged. He could not go on.

He also discovered a new passion as a writer. He published two articles on the front page of the *Chicago Defender*, the leading Black newspaper in the middle part of the country. He extolled the wonderful opportunities available to adventurous men willing to take up homesteads in South Dakota, and he

scolded young Black men reluctant to come out and tr
1913 Micheaux published his first novel, *The Conquest:
Story of a Negro Pioneer*. Published in Lincoln, Nebraska, it was
(and is) seen as his own story, very thinly disguised as fiction.
He published other novels, mostly based on his homesteading
experiences.

He also began making films, releasing his first silent film,
*The Homesteader*, in 1919, again telling the story of his own
experience. Micheaux became the most successful African
American filmmaker of the first half of the twentieth century.
His films, like his novels, drew from the deep well of his own
homesteading years.

Even though he left South Dakota after only a decade, he
returned to his homesteading experiences in films and novels
again and again. Not unlike the great American writer Willa
Cather, he found those times so powerful and rich that they
kept his creative juices flowing decades after he had left the
land. Micheaux died in 1951. In 1987 Hollywood honored this
South Dakota homesteader by placing a star with his name on
its iconic Walk of Fame. The star reads, "The Father of Independent Black Filmmaking."

Black migrants coming to homestead in the Great Plains generally found white neighbors to be friendly or, in some cases,
people who just left them alone to get on with their affairs.
As Nicodemus historian Charlotte Hinger noted, rural white
Kansans were more likely to give immigrants of all ethnic origins
a chance to prove themselves. For Kansans the most important factor was whether the newcomers could prevail against
the environmental odds. The same was mostly true for white
homesteaders elsewhere in the region.

Still, there were some racial clashes. At Nicodemus, in
Graham County, Kansas, nearby cattle ranchers and their

cowboys disliked any "dirt-busters" who upended the grass and fenced off the open range. Six separate times in 1878 they intentionally ran their herds over Black farmers' fields. One day the cowboys got irritated that Nicodemus people were watering their cattle in the South Solomon River, and they drove the Nicodemus cows away. But the Nicodemus men managed to capture one of the cowboys. They held him hostage until the cowboys returned their cows. The cowboys left them alone after the Black farmers, joined by some nearby white homesteaders, defended themselves a few times.

Black homesteader William P. Walker triggered the only serious incident at DeWitty when he had his homestead surveyed and fenced. Very soon, a white rancher whose spread lay next door, showed up irritated and accompanied by several tough cowhands. Walker sensed danger but remained calm.

"We know you had your claim surveyed," the rancher said, "and some of my ranch boundaries are over on your claim."

Walker jumped in before the man could say more. "Well, now, everything is all right, we can work out a way to settle things. Why don't you just pay me in hay for my land each year?"

The rancher, momentarily nonplussed, readily accepted this proposal. The tension evaporated, and he left with his men. Although on this occasion a white rancher had confronted a Black homesteader, the quarrel was more about access for grazing cattle than about racial differences, and it was peacefully settled with Walker maintaining his rights. DeWitty homesteaders recorded few other confrontations with surrounding ranchers.

The Black homesteaders who established Empire, in Goshen County, Wyoming, encountered overt racial hostility leading to the demise of their colony. Baseman Taylor, brother of community leader Rev. Russel Taylor, suffered from poverty and depression. By 1912 Russel saw that Baseman was becoming paranoid and aggressive, and he worried that Baseman had become a physical threat to Russel's family and to their neighbors. Russel asked a court to declare Baseman incompetent, expecting that his brother would be sent to Wyoming's State Insane Asylum in Evanston.

Goshen County sheriff's deputies took Baseman into custody, treating him roughly and injuring his head. Baseman began having seizures. Lacking a jail, the deputies took him to the Torrington Hotel. Baseman refused to keep quiet in the lobby, where the deputies repeatedly struck and brutalized him. Hotel guests and staff looked on in horror. Baseman continued to be loud and disruptive, so the deputies took him to an upstairs room. They shackled him to the bed and continued to torture him, trying to control him. At some point, they damaged his trachea. Baseman Taylor died after three days of beatings.

The county prosecutor refused to charge the deputies with any crime. The *Torrington Telegraph* wrote off Taylor's death as a result of his preexisting neurological condition. No one was held responsible, dispiriting the entire Empire colony. Combined with poor crops and internal disputes among homesteaders, the murder sank the colony.

Racial tension existed at Blackdom as well. As Black homesteader Roosevelt Boyer Sr. described, "At first whites didn't mind [the Black homesteaders]. They were all from the North and they soon all moved out and left the place to the [incoming] Southerners. They didn't like nobody. They was hard on us as they could be." And when Blackdom residents ventured into nearby Roswell, they encountered discrimination and hostility. Even so, Blackdom residents apparently did not suffer violence or the kind of intimidation that was so pervasive in the South.

Beyond scattered incidents, including Baseman Taylor's murder, relations between Black homesteaders and white neighbors were mostly positive and often mutually beneficial. At Nicodemus, residents established congenial relationships with the white community soon after it became clear to all that the Black colonists intended to stay and could defend themselves. And for the next decade, whites, ever the minority, operated businesses in the town and participated amicably in its social and cultural life.

At DeWitty, Black residents and white ranchers developed a mutually dependent and mutually beneficial economy. Most residents who worked off-farm found jobs at the nearby white ranches. The Hanna and Faulhaber families employed Black men as wranglers, handymen, and cooks, the Triple-L ranch hired Albert Riley as a farmhand, the Lee ranch employed William Ford. Chris Stith cooked on the Box T Ranch's chuck wagon during cattle drives, and at other times he and his wife Maggie both worked in the kitchen of the ranch house. DeWitty people relied on white ranchers to employ them so they could earn the cash they desperately needed. The ranchers benefited by employing trustworthy workers who, because they also owned land in the area, were more reliable and responsible than transient hands.

Similarly, at Dearfield, in Weld County, Colorado, cash-poor homesteaders hired themselves out to nearby ranchers. James Monroe Thomas was one serving as a farm hand. Colony leader O. T. Jackson noted in 1915 that the colony's main support came from employment by the white farmers and ranchers within ten or so miles of Dearfield. "This has been a great help to us and to them," Jackson wrote. "We have cooperated with each other by exchange of work, the use of tools and horses, sharing our food and fuel, until now we are like one large family."

Alice McDonald is the granddaughter of homesteaders at The Dry, a Black colony on the southeastern Colorado plains. The Dry survived from about 1915 to 1935. McDonald said The Dry was remarkably free of racial tension between Blacks and neighboring whites. "There was no strife and there was no racism. The people that came to The Dry depended on the white farmers and they were glad that they had come because they knew they knew how to farm and they knew they were willing to work."

McDonald described one incident when her father, Harvey Craig, was driving home late one night and his car broke down. He decided to walk the few miles to his home. The night was very dark. Electric power lines hadn't yet penetrated the rural areas, so there were no lights glowing from nearby farmhouses to reassure him.

After a time he saw a bright glow ahead of him. When he got closer, he saw it was a gathering of Ku Klux Klansmen. They were gathered in a circle, sitting on their horses. They wore white robes, high pointed hoods, and masks over their faces. Each held aloft a burning torch, producing the glow Harvey Craig had seen in the otherwise pitch-black darkness of the night. One of the Klansmen noticed the man walking by and rode over to him.

The Klansmen called out, "Harv, what do you need?"

Craig knew who the Klansman was by his voice, even though his face was obscured by the mask. He explained to the Klansman that his car had broken down and he was walking home.

The Klansman said, "I'll pick you up in the morning and take you to your car and get it started."

Just then another Klansman rode up and said, "Who's that?"

The first Klansman said, "Oh, it's Harv."

The second Klansman asked, "Does he need help?"

The first Klansman answered, "I told him I would help him tomorrow. Not to worry."

DeWitty descendant Joyceann Gray used the stories passed down in her family to write a novelized version of life in DeWitty called *Our DeWitty: And Now We Speak*. She puts these words in the mouth of Charlotte Walker, William P. Walker's second wife: "One really nice thing about living in this part of the country were those white folks living in and around Overton, Seneca and Brownlee. They came to help us get settled without having been asked."

Gray, in the voice of Walker, noted, "We went to school together at times and shared in games on Sunday afternoons. We had the best baseball team and played the best music and we always shared our meals after the games." She added, "I will forever be thankful for our part of the world because we felt safe and secure and our white neighbors supported that comradery. The racism if you want to call it that was subtle. Never causing either group a lot of concern. Both groups made adjustments to when and where necessary."

The relative lack of violence and the fact that they were largely left to themselves was a big advance for those who, in Gray's words, came in search of "most of all, peace." She added that what Black homesteaders most wanted was "the peace to make a living, peace to educate their children, peace to sit out on their porches and look over their land, with confidence that it was truly theirs, knowing that no one was coming over the next knoll to take and destroy!"

None of the Black colonies except Nicodemus survive, and Nicodemus is but a shadow of its former, robust self. A few Black farm families trace their origins to homesteading days, but most homesteaders appear to have sold out and moved on. Is the disappearance of these communities evidence that Black homesteading was a failure? Some consign the Black colonies to history's dustbin, labeling their residents as misguided agrarian migrants who fled unspeakable conditions in the South only to wind up on unsustainable and unrewarding farms in the Great Plains.

But neither Black homesteaders nor their descendants have seen it that way. Homesteaders like Henry Burden, William P. Walker, and James Monroe Thomas owned their own farms and saw their crops, livestock, and families grow. They must have felt an immense surge of pride in that accomplishment.

Over time the homesteaders came to see their farms as transitional spaces, places where they could escape and recover from the trauma of the South, earn livelihoods for themselves and their families, and educate their children for successful lives likely to be led elsewhere. Descendant Joyceann Gray noted that DeWitty was not built to last. She wrote that "the driving force behind every plow, every nail driven, every sod wall built was with one purpose in mind. Not to build a lasting farming town but to be the steppingstone for their children." Descendant Catherine Meehan Blount echoed Gray's assessment, adding, "[DeWitty] was meant to educate their children. DeWitty provided a better life for their children."

DeWitty homesteaders thus redefined the goals of their great venture. DeWitty would serve as a way station in a historic process that opened greater opportunities for succeeding generations to use their talents and pursue their dreams. As descendant Wayne Brown put it, "Education was the key. Some of the families say that DeWitty wasn't supposed to last for a long time, it lasted for thirty years, but it was a purchase. It was a purchase in American freedom. And in that freedom, they purchased education."

The homesteading generation's belief in education created the same Hobson's choice that so many farm families had to face. Children educated to become nurses, teachers, lawyers, pharmacists, insurance agents, doctors, or police officers do not in general return to carry the family farm into the future. To use their education, they have to leave home and farming. And to complete this bittersweet irony, their children's successes in

other occupations were exactly what the homesteader generation had hoped for them. In a phenomenon familiar in both
white and Black communities, the farming generation's deep
commitment to educating their children produced children
who were not, for the most part, interested in farming.

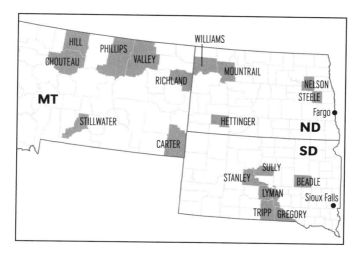

**Fig. 16.** Map of counties in South Dakota, North Dakota, and Montana mentioned in the text. Map by Katie Nieland.

# CHAPTER SEVEN

# The Twentieth-Century Land Rush

The United States suffered a severe bank panic in 1893 and descended into a terrible economic depression. It lasted from 1893 to 1897 and was often referred to as "the Great Depression" until the 1930s disaster displaced it. So too farmers in many Great Plains locations saw drought dry up their fields. Hard times for farmers indeed. Many joined the Populist movement, demanding relief from extortionate railroad freight rates, oppressive mortgage terms imposed by eastern finance companies, and the scarcity of currency due to both major parties' fealty to the punishing gold standard.

When the national economy and the weather improved at the end of the decade, national spirits rose. Once again, landless people, those renting farms or working as farmhands or simply dreaming of owning land, showed renewed interest in homesteading. They revived the dream of free land. But added to their hopes was a growing anxiety that the good land available for homesteading was quickly getting gobbled up. Maybe it was already gone; the opportunity to homestead seemed to be disappearing.

Oscar Micheaux, writing from his homestead in Gregory County, South Dakota, warned Black men back in Chicago that "Jews, Germans, Swedes, Arabs, Southern whites and Irish were all on hand to get land" and that the Blacks better come quick or the whites would get it all.

"Primarily a quarter section of land was the reason for almost everyone coming west" is how homesteader and newswoman Edith Ammons Kohl put it. "As people in the early pioneer days had talked of settling in Nebraska and Kansas and eastern Dakotas, they now talked about the country lying farther on—the western Dakotas, Wyoming, Montana, Colorado. Over the Midwest, the homestead idea was spreading rapidly to farm and hamlet and city."

Some called it Homestead Fever or Montana Fever, a malady that caused people, even those who made a comfortable living among friends in pleasant surroundings, to pull up stakes and strike out for the West to homestead. The new optimism, matched with a fear of missing out, unleashed a surge of new land seekers. Charles Bern, born in Sweden but comfortably settled in River Falls, Wisconsin, with his wife and three small children, felt the call. He worked as a sign and house painter, but he was already developing symptoms of lead poisoning from the paint, and his doctor advised him to change his occupation.

The doctor's advice fell on receptive ears because Bern was ready for a change. He and some friends made an exploratory trip to western North Dakota and liked what they saw. So in the winter of 1906–7 he sold the family's River Falls house and, with three other families, prepared to go west. On May 1, 1907, they stepped off the train in Hettinger County, North Dakota, eager to homestead.

The Bern family, like other homesteaders after the turn of the century, moved to the western extremes of the Great Plains. Hettinger County lies in the southwestern part of North Dakota, not far from Montana. The covered wagons were mostly gone. Rail lines with their spurs, like the one that carried the Bern family to the tiny town of Mott, extended far into the countryside and made travel to the homesteading regions easier and quicker. Still, there remained those difficult last few miles to reach one's claim.

Ida Ammons, searching in the Chamberlin, South Dakota, land office in 1907, found an open claim about thirty miles west of Pierre. It was in Lyman County. A man had previously filed on it, built a house there, and then abandoned it; so the land reverted to the government. Ida was delighted not only to find available land but to discover that the claim already had a house on it—free land *and* a free house! She and her sister Edith were young women who had come out from Illinois to make their futures, and Ida filed on the claim.

They paid a land locator twenty dollars to take them to their new home. They loaded their trunks and supplies into his old spring wagon. The sisters and their driver bumped across the raw prairie, "brown grass scorched and crackling from the sun. No trees to break the endless monotony or to provide a moment's respite from the sun." Finally, they stopped, the prairie stretching to the horizon in all directions and no neighbors in sight. The driver deposited the women and their goods at the door of the dwelling, turned his horses around, and drove off. Ida and Edith were left alone to start their new life.

Adelia Hawkins (later Sturm, later Glover) traveled west from New York in 1909, seeking opportunity with her mother and two brothers. They stopped for a time in Des Moines, where they all found jobs, and then they relocated to Minneapolis, again finding work. One day Adelia's brothers, William and Claire, announced they were going to Montana to homestead. Adelia did not want to go, because she liked her job in a real estate office and had just found a young man she was interested in. But her mother wanted to go with her boys. So in order not to break up the family, Adelia agreed to go too.

**Fig. 17.** Immigrant train, Great Northern Railway, circa 1910.
Drawing by Adam Edwards Mayhew.

The Great Northern Railroad offered special fares to settlers
moving west. On an "immigrant train" the reduced fare paid
for a boxcar in which passengers and their household goods,
farm implements, and livestock traveled all together. The
Hawkinses filled half the car with pots, dishes, clothes, and
furniture, the other half with livestock her brothers had bought
in Minneapolis. They arrived in the town of Big Sandy, Montana,
in February.

Adelia filed a 320-acre Enlarged Homestead claim in
Chouteau County, Montana, in 1912. Together with her
brothers' and mother's claims, the family controlled two full
sections. Snow closed the primitive roads that led out to their
claims, thirty-five miles across the prairie, so they stayed in town.

In April the brothers finally broke through the snowdrifts to
get to their land. They lived in a tent until they could build a

shack, and then the women joined them on the claim. Will and Claire broke some land, built corrals for the livestock, strung fencing, and dug a well. Adelia was lonely and described herself as "the only single girl within a radius of 25 miles." The family's social life was limited to visits to nearby ranches. They too had succumbed to Montana Fever.

Both sets of my grandparents joined this new wave of homesteading. Webster and Rosabell Edwards homesteaded in Mountrail County in western North Dakota in 1902. They had been renting a farm in Lakota, North Dakota, for some years and apparently had saved enough to go west on their own. Webster went first to file the claim and get ready for the arrival of the family. He took as much of the stock and machinery as he could manage, built a sod house, and planted a small garden. Then he came back to Lakota to collect my grandmother and their six small children.

They rode west on a Great Northern immigrant train. They traveled in the boxcar along with the farm machinery, household goods, and livestock. The train chugged west for a day or two, and then shunted the immigrant cars onto a siding so the men could water and exercise the animals and the women could prepare food and wash clothes. They passed through Devil's Lake, Rugby, and Minot. They got out at Stanley, a small village of fifty people only provisioned with a poorly stocked general store, a land office, and a pool hall. From there they traveled by wagon and on foot the four miles south to their claim. They had no nearby kin or friends.

My maternal grandparents, the Burlingames, also homesteaded in Mountrail County. They were part of a large family group, the Hageys—my grandmother was born a Hagey—who filed claims near each other in 1903. Eight Hageys, three Carcuffs, and three Arndts, all cousins or siblings or in-laws, filed claims in Brookbank and Sikes townships in the first decade of the new century. This was dry country that got only about fifteen inches of precipitation a year, good for growing wheat, rye, flax, and oats except in years of "drouth." The Hageys brought a dense network of kin ties to their rural neighborhood, a valuable resource for farming and psychological support, though not always without internal conflict.

Brookbank Township was a fine but ordinary stretch of prairie just north of the Missouri River, containing nothing special to make it distinctive. But like the rest of Mountrail County, it filled up quickly. Poor farmers and would-be farmers sensed that this was their opportunity to homestead on good land, and they were determined not to be left out. In Brookbank, one lonely homesteader filed a claim in 1892, but starting in 1900 claimants flooded in. In the following twelve years, from 1900 to 1911, settlers filed 127 homestead claims, filling up the prairie and leaving little unclaimed land. Those 127 claims amounted to 82 percent of all claims filed in the township. The last claim was filed in 1920.

The rush to claim land in Brookbank was not exceptional. Mountrail, which hadn't yet separated from Ward County, had fewer than three hundred non-Native residents in 1900. By 1910 it contained 8,491 people, nearly all of them homesteaders. By 1920 it had grown again, to 12,140 residents. The land maps showed nearly all sections had been claimed. And the whole state was growing like Mountrail—North Dakota's population doubled between 1900 and 1920.

For some, the experience was more like a race. Congress opened to settlement the "Unassigned Lands," a two-million-acre tract in the middle of Indian Territory (what would become Oklahoma). The GLO announced that non-Natives could enter the area at noon on April 22, 1889, to begin filing claims. Fifty thousand impatient land seekers gathered on the tract's borders, ready to pounce. Undermanned army troopers tried to restrain them but with mixed success. Some claimants, later known as "Sooners," cheated by getting an early start.

When the signal sounded, thousands rushed in from all sides of the Unassigned Lands in a frantic, frenzied race to be first to stake claims. The land rush created chaos, confusion, trickery, and violence. Eager land seekers filed some eleven thousand homestead claims within a week.

The scene was different in South Dakota. In 1904 President Theodore Roosevelt opened 385,000 acres of "surplus" Rosebud Reservation land to homesteading, enough room to accommodate 2,400 homesteads. The government was still embarrassed by the chaotic fiasco of the Oklahoma land run. This time it decided to choose winners by lottery. Eligible individuals who wanted land were required to travel to tiny Chamberlain, South Dakota, or one of the other registration towns and put in their applications in person between 9:00 a.m. on July 5 and 6:00 p.m. on July 23.

It created a frenzy. Right up to the deadline, five or six special trains a day, overloaded with hundreds of land seekers, arrived to spill out their human cargo. Oscar Micheaux and a future U.S. president were among them. In total, 107,408 hopefuls submitted applications. Towns put up tents to accommodate the newcomers, but they were grossly inadequate to house the excited crowds. Foresighted travelers brought their own small tents, which they erected all around the outskirts. But most visitors were left to shelter in the crowded saloons.

Registrants added their sealed application envelopes to a growing pile, from which GLO officials would later select winners at random. The officials assigned a number to each application they selected. Winners would choose their homesteads in the order in which their applications had been drawn. When enough homesteaders had entered claims to exhaust the land available, the remaining applicants were out of luck. Losers.

On Thursday, July 28, officials in Chamberlain, county seat of Brule County, South Dakota, drew out the winning submissions. Superintendent James Witten, in charge of the GLO's opening of Indian lands, called out the winners' names. Most of the applicants chosen had already gone home and would be notified by mail. The watching crowd cheered the first winner present, a farmer from Oklahoma, and demanded a speech. Then they waited, tense and hopeful.

Applicants whose envelopes were drawn early in the process and thus given low numbers went away ecstatic. Those with middling numbers departed still hopeful, believing that some with lower numbers might not in fact show up to claim their land. Those who drew high numbers or who did not have their envelopes drawn at all knew they had lost, and they left with depressed spirits.

Harry Truman, a twenty-seven-year-old failed Missouri farmer, did not have his number drawn that day. "I could never draw anything," he groused to his fiancée, Bess Wallace. In his case failure to become a South Dakota homesteader worked out pretty well. Heinrich Koenig, a Lutheran pastor from Canova, South Dakota, was an ecstatic winner, though as we will see, his success proved to be the cause of his life's greatest tragedy.

In 1908 President Roosevelt opened another 828,000 acres of Rosebud Reservation land, winners again to be chosen in a lottery. The GLO received 114,769 applications for the roughly five thousand available homesteads. At Dallas, platted just the year before and already boasting a population of 1,277, thirty-four carloads of land seekers arrived between midnight and daybreak on the first day of registration. The little hamlet of Presho, one of the ancillary registration stations, woke (in the words of one observer) "to find a great drove of tenderfeet stampeding down its little Main Street. They thundered down the board sidewalk and milled in the middle of the road, kicking

**Fig. 18.** Land seekers in Gregory, South Dakota. They flooded in to file their registrations for a lottery in opening of Rosebud Reservation lands, October 1, 1909. Legend on photo reads, "LINE UP OF ENTRYMEN FOR GENERAL FILING ON TRIPP CO. LANDS, OCT. 1st '09 U.S. LAND OFFICE, GREGORY, S.D." Permission of *South Dakota Magazine.*

up dust like a herd of range cattle as they went." And the Presho crowd was only the spray cast by the tidal wave that landed at Gregory, the primary registration site.

Such large crowds attracted pickpockets, hustlers, confidence men, thieves, and women selling sandwiches and other services. A local newspaper reported that "while a vast majority of the land seekers are legitimate settlers, actuated by the honest impulse to secure a home for themselves and families . . . there are not lacking adventurers, gamblers and fakirs [looking] to pick up a little 'easy money.'"

On Monday, October 19 GLO agents in Gregory dumped out all the sealed envelopes in the barrels onto a platform, ostentatiously mixed them up with rakes and hoes, and put them into a giant wheel. Two small girls, blindfolded, drew out the envelopes. Hopefuls in the tense crowd watched as the girls drew more names from the wheel and officials announced the lucky winners. The GLO mailed notifications to the winners and gave them specific times to make their selection. It informed Mary Bartels, "You must on April 9, 1909, at 1:40 o'clock or as soon thereafter as your name is called file your homestead application [at] the United States land office located at Gregory, S. Dak., [or] all rights under your number will be forfeited."

Unlike participants in the dramatic Oklahoma land runs or Rosebud lotteries, most Great Plains homesteaders filtered into the region alone or with their relatives and friends to claim their land. Some came in small affiliated groups. When land seekers learned that a region like Brookbank Township became available, they tended to fill it quickly. Sections sixteen and thirty-six in every township were off-limits, held out as "school lands." But in the other thirty-four sections of a township, homesteaders rushed in and left little land unclaimed, except sometimes small patches of unusable land.

Elizabeth Corey grew up on a farm in Iowa. Her parents and six siblings—Bess was the oldest—crowded into their small four-room house. Her parents not so subtly goaded Bess to move out and relieve them of supporting her. A nearby school district hired her in 1905, at age seventeen, as its teacher. Single women's career prospects were mainly limited to being teachers, nurses, and housemaids, but Bess wanted more. She was excited by the fulsome stories put out by the railroads and others describing the wonderful opportunities to homestead in South Dakota. She knew that a claimant had to be twenty-one to homestead, so she waited.

When she came of age, Bess packed her few belongings and rode the Northwestern Railway to South Dakota. Her plan was to stake her claim, find a teaching job, and use her wages to hire men to build her a shack and break the required ten acres of prairie sod. She got out at a two-story depot, newly painted red, whose board sign declared it to be Midland. It was the early morning hours of June 3, 1909. The town still slept, no one moving about in the dark.

How to find a good claim? The plats and maps at the local land office often lagged far behind recording claims, making land appear available when it was not. So Corey depended on new acquaintances she made in South Dakota to steer her to a claim. She chatted up the night agent at the train station while she waited for Midland to wake up. He had already filed his claim, and he suggested there was more land near his entry. Corey didn't pursue that lead.

She met another young Iowa woman, Lida Smith, who had relatives running a South Dakota ranch. The rancher's son, Will Scarborough, helped them locate two possible claims near the ranch. Lida filed on the first, but when Bess tried to claim the second, she made an unwelcome discovery: "One of those long legged evil eyed monsters called men had beat me to the land office and got my claim." She next found a claim that a man named Carlson was willing to relinquish, but she refused to pay his asking price.

Finally, in early August 1909, Bess "took a half a day off [work] and went over to Pierre and talked to a land man." That man was M. B. Hastings, a professional land locator. He promised her a better claim than the Carlson place, and after a daylong trip bumping over the prairie in a horse-drawn wagon, she agreed. She would be buying a relinquishment.

Bess filed on the 160-acre tract in Stanley County, South Dakota. But she was nervous enough about the legality of the relinquishment that she wrote her mother back in Iowa to "holler [celebrate] all you want to but don't tell anyone for a few wks. till I get my receipt please." She needn't have worried—Bess got her official notice that her filing had been accepted. She too was now a homesteader.

As the press of land seekers continued, newcomers were pushed to increasingly marginal lands. Central South Dakota, western North Dakota, and eastern Montana turned out to be excellent wheat country, and they remain bountiful producing regions down to the present. They are always vulnerable to drought but produce ample crops in normal years.

Claimants moved further west, into central Montana, the eastern plains of Wyoming and Colorado, the Nebraska sandhills, and even eastern New Mexico. These regions could be productive in "wet" years, but during too many years sparse rain left the fields too dry for farmers to prosper. Today, except where farmers can use center-pivot irrigation, they use these areas mainly for grazing, not for field crops.

Montana was the epicenter of the late homesteading rush. Land seekers flooded its eastern plains, swayed by exaggerated promotions by railroads and local and state development boards. Many filed 320-acre claims under the new (1909) Enlarged Homestead Act.

Charles Hawkins arrived in Culbertson, Roosevelt County, in 1904. He had grown up in Sweden as Kyrle Hakkansson but anglicized his name on arrival in the United States. He spent eight years working as a fur dresser before deciding to take up the government's offer of free land. At age twenty-four he filed on a 160-acre claim. Four years later, his fiancée, Ella Flink, an eighteen-year-old housemaid in Saint Paul, joined him.

Charles broke prairie land for fields and planted flax and wheat. Ella planted a large garden, cared for cows and chickens, and helped harvest the wheat. She endured six pregnancies in twelve years, delivering all six babies at home. Three of her children died at birth. Her granddaughter believes those deaths caused her to be uninterested in and cold to her youngest child, a daughter, who survived.

The Hawkins family did well during the wetter years, from 1910 to 1917, seven years of plenty. Charles proved up his claim in 1912. But they suffered during the next seven, lean years. Although war in Europe caused crop prices to shoot up, farmers in eastern Montana faced drought and poor crop yields. Then in 1921 crop prices collapsed, sending farm country into depression even before the Great Depression.

William Alexander lived in Morristown, Minnesota. The forty-six-year-old worked as the local superintendent of schools, and his wife Mary taught in the same schools. In 1913 he decided to throw over his career as an educator and become a homesteader—he had contracted a bad case of Montana Fever. He moved to Richland County in eastern Montana, bringing along Mary and their two children, ages five and three. But Alexander fell into the trap that hobbled so many novice farmers—he chose his claim for its sweeping views and failed to notice its thin and rocky soils.

The Alexanders struggled even during the good years. William's crops did poorly. Mary, a teacher at heart, learned to pick up cow patties for fuel and crush the bedbugs brought in with the pine boards William used to build their shack.

When the hard times at the end of the decade came, Mary picked up and left. She took their daughter with her and moved seven miles away, where she found a job teaching in a one-room schoolhouse. She left their son to be raised by his father on the claim. Eventually William gave up, too, joining the great number of Montana land seekers who wound up landless. He sold his claim to neighbors.

Charles and Ella Hawkins somehow held on. They watched as their neighbors struggled and became discouraged, fell deeper into poverty, their fields dried up except for Russian thistle.

The Hawkinses added to their holdings, taking over farms with foreclosed mortgages or farms that had simply been abandoned, farms whose owners had fled to California. Though they led a hardscrabble life of toil and meager rewards, Charles and Ella persisted. Charles farmed until he was eighty-nine.

The great Montana land rush generated the most homestead claims in the hundred-year history of the Homestead Act. In just the five years from 1914 to 1918, Montana homesteaders proved up 62,625 claims, becoming owners of more than thirteen million acres. The 1917 total (14,891 claims) and 1918 total (14,178) were the largest for any state in one year ever. For some, like the Alexanders, it proved to be a hard life that ended with the loss of their land. For others, like the Hawkinses, it became the foundation for a multigenerational farm, purchased with toil, hardship, and sacrifice.

# CHAPTER EIGHT

# Life on the Twentieth-Century Homestead

In the new century, homesteading moved west and was transformed. Railroads built out their networks of branch and spur lines, reaching their peak of Great Plains trackage around 1916. Grain companies built elevators, adding the iconic vertical element to the otherwise horizontal and featureless landscape.

Agricultural technology progressed. Breaking the prairie became easier with the arrival of the huge coal-fed steam tractors. Farmers who could afford to hire them (many could not) brought the big machines and their drivers in to turn their sod. And harvesting wheat and other small grains also changed. Enormous threshing machines, like monstrous ants from the horror movie *Them!*, crept up from Oklahoma to the Dakotas as the grain ripened. Tended by a gang of twenty or more men, they devoured the wheat shocks and spit out the golden harvest.

Still, aside from breaking and threshing, much else about the homestead remained unchanged. Virtually all farmers continued to depend on horses or oxen to power their field machinery. They hauled their harvest to elevators in horse-drawn farm wagons. More lumber came into the region by rail than had before, but many homesteaders continued to build with sod.

Electric and telephone lines had revolutionized urban life, but they would not reach Great Plains farmhouses for another generation or two. Congress passed President Franklin

Roosevelt's Rural Electrification Act in 1936, but in most areas it was only much later that line crews actually showed up to install the familiar wooden poles that run alongside rural roads and string wire on them. Anders and Gudrun Svendsbye didn't get electric power on their Williams County, North Dakota, farm until 1949.

Farm families instead relied on kerosene lamps for light and burned scrap wood or lignite in their cook stoves for heat. They canned to preserve food and hand-cranked their milk separators. Most women gave birth assisted by midwives, not doctors.

My Edwards grandparents built sod houses on the western Dakota prairie in 1902. The small size of their house, only ten by fourteen feet and crowded with six children, must have made living difficult and tense; there certainly was no privacy for intimacy.

Webster lined the inside walls with wide boards and inserted two windows, each just twenty inches square, in the end wall opposite the door. The family heated the house with a small cast-iron cook stove. The parents had a real bed, while the children slept on cots that folded up on the wall during the day. On another wall they placed the washstand, holding a pail of water with its long dipper and a basin for the men to wash up in when they came in from the fields. They filled the interior space with a small table and two chairs, prizes brought out from Illinois.

In summer they moved the washstand and other items outside into the shade of the house, and they did as much cooking, eating, laundry, and relaxing outdoors as weather permitted. But during the long winters they were stuck inside. Little wonder, then, that Rosabell lasted only seven years before she fled to town. Ostensibly, she left to watch over the older children as they attended town schools, but her departure deepened a rift with Webster that never healed. They later divorced, an act so shameful for the family my father would never speak of it afterward.

My Burlingame grandparents homesteaded in 1903 and also built with sod. Frankie, a small, determined figure, was one of America's original clean freaks. She insisted that William plaster the inside walls with a mixture of lime and ash to make the interior brighter and the walls scrubbable. She relentlessly battled the dirt blown in by the unceasing prairie wind, and every day she got down on her hands and knees to scrub the board floor. They lived on their farm for twenty-two years, but in 1925 the hard times and my grandmother's abhorrence of dirt caused them to move to town. They then lived in a proper frame house, but my grandfather never reconciled to giving up his land.

Sod houses with their thick walls were said to be cooler in summer and warmer in winter than poorly insulated frame houses. But they weren't perfect. For one thing, they were crowded. A few settlers built larger sod structures. Charles and Rosetta Speese in Empire, Wyoming, built a five-room sod house. Isadore Haumont, a Belgian who homesteaded in Custer County, Nebraska, built a two-story sod "castle" with round turrets at the corners; it stood nineteen feet high.

But these were rare exceptions, and most soddies were cramped. They afforded almost no privacy for either reflection or intimacy. Ava Speese Day described her parents' sod home in the Cherry County, Nebraska, sandhills: "The folks' bed and dresser were in the southeast corner. Behind the door [to the outside] was a high cupboard. The north end was the kids' beds with the chiffonier [a high dresser with a mirror] as a divider. A window in the north wall later became the door to a lean-to kitchen. Between the beds was space for table and chairs, cook stove, heater, and the organ." And she added, "We had two big problems, the dirt and the flies."

Sod houses persisted well into the twentieth century, but gradually homesteaders turned to frame buildings. Across the northern plains, many homesteaders initially staked their claims using tar paper shacks. They could construct these flimsy buildings quickly and cheaply, with their two-by-four studs and board sheathing. They covered the roof and exterior walls with tar paper in a vain attempt to keep out rain, wind, snow, and cold. They stuck balled-up newspapers between the studs for insulation.

The Ammons sisters were overjoyed when, in the land office, they discovered their claim already had a house on it. But delight turned to disappointment when they saw it. It turned out to be a shack that "looked like a large but none too substantial packing-box tossed haphazardly on the prairie." It was ten by twelve feet and consisted of one room. Made of wide boards, the whole structure was protected from the prairie's violent storms by a thin layer of tar paper. "It looked as if the first wind would pick it up and send it flying through the air."

In 1909 the young South Dakota homesteader Elizabeth Corey hired Grant Stone, head of the family she initially boarded with, to build a shack on her nearby claim. It took him three days of work, for which he charged twenty cents per hour. Including the forty dollars for lumber, six or seven dollars for labor, and a few other purchased items, she paid about fifty dollars for the house, which she called "a dandy little home." She did insist that her cellar have board walls to keep the rattlesnakes out.

As cozy as her house might have been, Corey had to scramble to find water for her needs. Her claim contained no stream or pond. When she first settled, she filled buckets at a neighbor's pond and carried them home. "It isn't half mile but it gets heavy just the same," she wrote her mother. When she walked over to visit the Stone family, she sometimes filled a pail with water and carried it the mile and a half home. In winter Corey got water by melting snow.

After a year, she hired Stone to construct a cistern. She added gutters and downspouts to her roof to catch rainwater and divert it into the cistern. And each winter Stone and Bess's brother took a team and wagon to the river, cut blocks of ice, and packed them into the cistern. During spring and summer, the ice would melt, supplying her with fresh water.

Later, she had men build a small dam in a gully. Still, all these measures required work, caused her to be frugal in water use, and created anxiety when rains failed and water in the cistern dipped low.

Heinrich Koenig was thrilled when he won the lottery for Rosebud land. It seemed literally sent from God.

Koenig was a Lutheran pastor serving a rural German congregation. His $500 per year salary, supplemented by parishioners' gifts of eggs, butter, and other supplies, was enough to support him, his wife Martha, and their five children. But Koenig worried that he wouldn't have money for retirement. So when he heard about President Roosevelt's opening of Rosebud Reservation land to homesteading and the GLO's 1908 lottery, he acted. He put in his application.

Amazingly, he won! Humans worry; God provides. Perhaps Koenig had sermonized on Matthew 6:26, "Look at the birds of the air, for they neither sow nor reap nor gather into barns; yet your heavenly Father feeds them. Are you not of more value than they?" Koenig's winning ticket gave him the right to claim 160 acres near Ideal in Tripp County, South Dakota. He soon resigned his pastorship.

In 1910 the family loaded their livestock, household goods, and themselves aboard an immigrant train. They took it as far as Kennebec, then reloaded their goods into a wagon. They jolted over the last forty miles across empty prairie to their claim. They built a twelve-by-fourteen-foot shack, dug a root cellar, and planted a garden. Heinrich broke sod for a field.

Water was a problem. At first they hauled water from the White River, three miles away. But it wasn't good for human consumption, so they came to rely on a nearby spring. They also collected rainwater. To provide a long-term solution, Heinrich constructed a dam about three hundred yards from the house. The next summer wonderfully heavy rains filled the reservoir, creating a substantial pond behind the dam.

On a sunny morning in July 1911, the two oldest Koenig children, Gustav and Frieda, built a raft out of scrap lumber and launched it into the pond. The other three children played on the bank. At some point the raft capsized. Neither Gustav nor Frieda knew how to swim. Hulda, on the bank, plunged in to save her siblings, but all three children drowned.

The neighbors gathered, they dug three graves, and the bodies were washed and dressed. A friend rode in to Gregory, forty miles away, and retrieved three small caskets. The family buried the children and placed a headstone at their graves. The children's names and birthdates were cut into the stone, and then, in German, is the awful notation that all three children died on July 24, 1911.

Martha was inconsolable. Whenever she went outside, she saw the graves. She cried a lot. Even the birth of their sixth child did not raise her spirits. She longed to return to Minnesota or Iowa to get away from the prairie.

Koenig understood his wife's unhappiness. He appealed to church officials, and some weeks later they informed him that St. John's Lutheran Church in Aikin, Minnesota, had called him to their pastorate. He disposed of the farm machinery, livestock, and other possessions and sold the farm. They moved to Aikin. His winning lottery ticket had led to the saddest day in their lives.

**Fig. 19.** Minneapolis Threshing Company's coal-fueled steam tractor pulling plow (John Deere 24-bottom) in virgin sod on the Jack Anderson homestead, Dickey County, North Dakota, 1910. Permission of Institute for Regional Studies Archive Collection, North Dakota State University Archives.

Homesteaders who did not own draft animals or had animals not robust enough for breaking, as well as solo women homesteaders, hired someone to do the breaking for them. In 1909 Elizabeth Corey advised her brother, who was considering coming out from Iowa to homestead, that he could have his land broken for four dollars per acre. Ruth Giles Fischer homesteaded by herself in Chouteau County, Montana, in 1917. She got her claim broken for between $5.00 and $6.50 an acre. Sometimes the arrangement went further: Marion Chausse was a solo homesteader in Carter County, Montana, in 1914. She needed to have her claim broken, so she hired her neighbor Paul Pettis to do it. But as she wrote later, "We finally decided he needed a cook and I needed a farmer." So they got married.

Steam-driven tractors appeared early in the twentieth century. These enormous machines generated enough power to pull multiple-blade plows through the tough sod. The accompanying photo shows homesteader Jack Anderson's Minneapolis Threshing Company steam tractor pulling a John Deere twenty-four-blade plow through virgin sod in Dickey County, North Dakota. Such machines could break many more acres each day than a man with a team and breaking plow. But they required great quantities of coal to fuel them.

In 1911 Oscar Micheaux hired a man with a steam engine to break two hundred acres of his Tripp County, South Dakota, land, far from his home farm in Gregory County. Micheaux was required to haul four tons of coal to feed the machine. John McGruder, in Sully County, South Dakota, owned a big steam tractor and used it to break his own prairie and bust sod for other homesteaders. But after using ten wagonloads of coal breaking a field, it would take a further full wagonload of coal just to get the tractor back home.

Homesteaders found themselves in an isolated world largely limited to nearby neighbors, so their local community became a key part of their lives, for good or ill. Some homesteaders, like the Hageys and Berns, migrated with relatives or friends, bringing the rudiments of community with them. Some settled in ethnic communities. Many Norwegians, Finns, Swedes, Moravians, Bohemians, and others brought traditions and customs with them, and they were sustained by church, school, holidays, and community festivals.

Other neighborhoods were more diverse, and neighbors needed to learn how to get along (or not). Charles Bern had been born in Sweden. In section twenty of Cannon Ball township in Hettinger County, North Dakota, he lived alongside an Irishman, a Holland-born father and his son, and a native-born American. Beyond his section, he had neighbors from many ethnic backgrounds and religions with whom his family needed to collaborate. What they shared were the challenges of homesteading.

They were brought together by the immediate tasks they faced: keeping the roads cleared in winter, organizing a school, rounding up stray cattle, building a church. Threshing always required big crews, and every man in the neighborhood had a direct stake in helping out, knowing he would need the others' help when it came time to thresh his own grain.

Women cooperated, too, because the big threshing crew, after long hours of hard physical labor, came inside with enormous appetites. Women had to be up long before the crew started work, baking bread and biscuits and preparing breakfast; and in the evening they retired after the men, washing dishes and pots and pans and getting things ready for the next morning.

Threshing was a time of peak energy and camaraderie but also extremely hard work. At other times, homesteaders depended on their neighbors for other valued exchanges, including socializing and entertaining, organizing dances and trading visits on Sundays.

Rural neighbors came together soon after their arrival on their claims to open a school. State education commissioners had taken an increasing role in stimulating and setting standards for rural schools, but the primary job of organizing them remained with the farm families themselves. The Norwegian immigrants who homesteaded in Williams County, North Dakota, opened schools as soon as they began breaking ground. The first school near Wildrose began in 1904 with six students; it met in the granary on Martin Walstad's homestead. A school near McGregor (the town itself didn't yet exist) opened in 1905 in a rented sixteen-by-twenty homestead shack.

Schools adopted different schedules for when and how long they were open. Because children's labor was needed on the farm during the active months from April to October, families kept the schools open mainly in winter. Children walked to school during the worst months of cold and snow. Still, attendance records show most students attended regularly.

Elizabeth Corey moved to central South Dakota to homestead confident she could find employment as a teacher. She was right. Rural schools in Stanley County were already organized, despite its recent settlement, and she had her choice of openings. In 1909 she accepted a teaching post near her claim and boarded with the Stone family, who became her long-time friends.

Families sometimes came into conflict with county or state officials over which language would be used in school. The dilemma regarding whether to keep the old ways or adopt new American ones erupted in the dispute over naming the township where Anders and Gudrun Svendsbye filed their claim in Williams County, North Dakota. Homesteader C. J. Helle had migrated from Stordahl, a community near Trondheim, Norway. He connived with county commissioners to name their area Stordahl Township. But twenty-five of his neighbors, most of them also Norwegians, descended on his homestead to object. Helle got the message, and commissioners adopted the name Big Meadow Township.

Schools became a flashpoint for these language tensions. In areas settled by Norwegians, parents who only or mainly spoke Norwegian tended to hire Norwegian-speaking teachers. They wanted instruction in a language they could understand, and they wanted the schools to help transmit Norwegian culture to the children. German settlers wanted their children to be instructed in German. In most areas parents could decide the issue themselves, although when children graduated from the local one-room schoolhouse and went to town for high school, they were taught in English. There the rural students' limited English worked against them.

This system came apart during World War I and afterward when officials banned instruction in German. In 1919 Nebraska passed the Siman Act, which prohibited schools from using German to instruct pupils. Public sentiment turned against any non-English instruction and cast a cloud of suspicion over any "un-American" schools.

Neighbors also came together to build churches. In Protestant communities, churches tended to be simple and stark, fortunate because fierce denominational differences mandated separate churches. Neighbors usually started meeting in someone's home, the group later evolving into a congregation. In 1911 Russell Taylor organized Grace Presbyterian Church in the Black homesteader colony of Empire in Goshen County, Wyoming. It first met in congregants' homes, then moved to the town's new school when it was built. Finally, in 1915, the congregation constructed its own church building.

Typically, a small local congregation could not afford to hire a full-time pastor, so it shared a pastor with churches in other rural neighborhoods—the man making a circuit on Sundays or even holding services on alternating Sundays. Grace Presbyterian was lucky, because Taylor's salary was paid by the Wyoming Presbytery's Board of Home Missions. This arrangement relieved his cash-poor congregants from having to tithe to support him. Most rural congregations with few members struggled to recruit and retain their pastors.

In areas with significant Catholic believers, the Church constructed more elaborate edifices, subsidized by wealthier dioceses. But parishioners usually had to travel farther to go to confession and attend mass.

Homesteaders in the twentieth century, even those in remote areas, enjoyed much greater and easier communication with the outside world than had their nineteenth-century counterparts. Railroads came nearer and state roads improved, making it easier to receive goods and visit relatives. But the major contributor to improving rural life was the Post Office.

Congress passed Rural Free Delivery in 1896, bringing the mailman to farms, and it added Parcel Post delivery of packages in 1903. Direct delivery of mail had long been the standard in cities, but this was a new service for rural residents. The Post Office was slow in hiring drivers and developing routes, but by 1910 or so the system served most rural areas. Patrons could now receive and send mail right at the mailboxes mounted on posts at the end of their driveways.

Many rural residents watched for the telltale sign that the carrier's car was approaching—in summer, the dust cloud billowing out behind his car on the gravel road; in winter, the vehicle's dark shape outlined against the blank white fields of snow. They would hustle out to have a brief chat with the carrier.

My father, Roy Edwards, carried the mail for thirty-three years to 120 farm families in Mountrail County, North Dakota. He knew the families depended on him, sometimes running out of groceries in midwinter or needing him to call Dr. Flath to come and assist with a baby that was coming. He considered his post a solemn public trust requiring that he reach these families, regardless of weather. He modified a Model A, putting tractor tires on the back axle so that, in winter, he could bust through the three-foot snowdrifts that often blocked the roads.

Roy's car might have been the only one to pass by a family's farm that day or even that week, so his arrival was an event. Families welcomed him because he would spend two or three minutes chatting. As the farmer or his wife leaned against his car, Roy relayed the latest town news, dissected the previous evening's loss by the St. Louis Cardinals, visited about the weather—anything that broke up the monotony and loneliness of farm life. Much as farmers or their wives wanted to hear gossip about others from Roy ("Why is Strobeck's wife staying so long in California?"), they depended on him to keep their *own* affairs private. A few people liked to linger for longer conversations, forcing Roy to say three or four awkward goodbyes before he could extract himself and drive on to the next farm.

Rural delivery brought letters; postcards; newspapers; magazines; and (most importantly) catalogs from Sears, Roebuck and Montgomery Ward. The catalogs opened the door to a cornucopia that earlier homesteaders had done without—clothes patterns, tools, baby chicks, seeds, fruit, new boots, tinned foods, patent medicines, and all manner of other goods. Of course, seeing an item in the catalog didn't mean the typically cash-strapped families could afford to buy it. Even so, it greatly widened the possibilities for consumption.

Neighbors did not always get along, despite their shared needs, even when they were relatives or belonged to the same church. Minor disputes over chronically failing to maintain a fence line or forgetting to return a borrowed tool could fester into long-running feuds. Among the Hagey clan, Charlie Arndt was seen as hard to work with, tight with a dollar, and not quick to help others. In the Berns' neighborhood, neighbors fought over school matters, parents wanting the school to be located near their own homesteads to make it easier for their children to walk to school and possibly also to enhance the value of their land.

Unfriendly neighbors hounded the Black homesteaders at Empire in Goshen County, Wyoming. They were goaded on by the nasty racism of the nearby town of Torrington. One white rancher, Yorick Nichols, repeatedly sued members of the Speese family (who were Black), alleging all sorts of theft and bad dealings. He often found support in the Torrington court of biased justice of the peace James Jackson.

**Fig. 20.** James Stevenson family and homestead shack in the ominously named community of Gumbo Flats, Judith Basin County, Montana, 1908. Montana State Library.

For neighbors who weren't feuding, nothing brought them together faster than a disaster. Winter sent the mercury to thirty or forty below and brought disorienting blizzards and impassable snow drifts, and it always posed special dangers. But other seasons had their dangers too. The year 1910 looked to be promising for the Berns. They had built their house and outbuildings and had a flourishing garden. Most of their land was broken and planted with wheat. The weather the previous year had been excellent, producing a bumper crop—so much so that Charles had built a new granary to hold the new crop.

On March 23 Charles went into town to complete a sign-painting job and earn extra cash, which was always welcome. The two older children went off to school. About noon his wife, Olive, home with the baby, went outside to try to find a broach she had dropped. To her horror she discovered a violent prairie fire coming directly at her. The tall grass and a sixty-mile-per-hour wind fueled a high wall of flames.

She grabbed baby Ivan and ran to a bend in the creek bed, standing at the edge of the water. They watched the fire's terrible path of destruction. Sparks driven by the heavy wind first lit the haystacks in the pasture and then sent up burning torches of loose straw which flew toward the buildings. The fire set all the buildings—the house and barn and outbuildings—on fire at once. Everything quickly burned to the ground, and then the fire moved on.

Charles, in town, grew frantic when he saw the smoke. He rushed home, sick with fear that he had lost his entire family. He found Olive and Ivan by the creek, sooty and terrified but alive. The older children were safe at school, because the fire had been unable to jump a new railroad grade and so did not burn the schoolhouse.

But the fire destroyed everything the Berns owned—the house and all its belongings, including clothes, dishes, pans, toys, everything. The barn and other buildings were all burned to the ground. The garden and crops, including the plentiful 1909 harvest stored in the granary, all lost. The calves in the barn, the cattle in the field, the chickens, the house cat—all killed. The horses were so badly burned they had to be shot. All the farm implements were ruined, the iron parts twisted beyond repair by the intense heat and the wooden handles burned. Everything was gone.

The Bern family now faced starting over from scratch, their three years' hard labor burned up and gone in less than an hour. Their neighbors came to their support. The Ellertson family took in the family's eleven-year-old daughter, Enid. The Banner family gave shelter to Olive and the two younger boys. Ethel Rumph, a young homesteader whose claim lay just a mile from the burned-over Bern place, offered them her shack to live in while they reconstructed their lives. The Berns were extremely grateful for their neighbors' generosity, and they would have been homeless and destitute without it.

Yet Charles and Olive knew that rebuilding their farm lay squarely on their own shoulders. Despite the terrible shock of the fire and the setback to their dreams, the Berns still had their land as a foundation to build on. They started over.

They had few alternatives to rebuilding, but they may have been committed to the land because it was so beautiful as well as productive. Daughter Enid later remembered her days as a twelve-year-old languidly tending the cows as they grazed: "I loved the prairies. . . . The broad expanse of grassy plains, bounded only by buttes and hills in the distance, had a special charm. . . . The singing of the meadow larks and the whistling of the gophers set the mood for the day, and countless discoveries in nature filled me with untold pleasure." She treasured "The birds' nests, each with its own particular kind of eggs, the various flowers, pretty stones, turtle eggs found in the walls of a cutbank, and even the snakes that startled me so. I learned to know where all these things could be found. . . . I [gazed] out over a view that was so beautiful as to be painful, trying to fix the scene in my mind so firmly that I would never forget it."

Homesteading brought incredible highs: the beauty of the land, the building of a future by poor people who had never thought they had a future, the soaring pride of accomplishment. But it came with disappointment, too, and with devastating setbacks and tragedy.

# CHAPTER NINE

# Homesteading Women

Homesteaders were nearly as likely to be women as men. Their names have already appeared throughout earlier chapters, but the way women homesteaded was usually distinct from the way men homesteaded and so deserves a discussion of its own.

Undoubtedly the most common way women homesteaded was as wives, part of a team with their husbands. In 1873 when Henry and Rosie Ise drove their wagon and led their cows to Henry's claim in Osborne County, Kansas, Rosie was entering into a life-changing experience as fully as Henry was. They followed gender-defined and gender-constrained roles, to be sure, although even here their circumstances caused them to be flexible. On the trip out, they traded jobs back and forth, sometimes Rosie driving the wagon and other times herding the cattle.

And when they set up their farm, Rosie and Henry both made crucial, though different, contributions to the farm's success. Rosie turned out to have far more steel in her backbone than her gentle and reflective husband. One day Jake Hardtarfer, a weaselly sort who farmed a claim across the river from the Ises, unexpectedly visited Henry when Rosie was away. Hardtarfer played on Henry's impulse to be generous to neighbors, and he persuaded Henry to cosign a $200 loan so Hardtarfer could buy a team.

When Rosie learned about it, she immediately recognized that it was a huge mistake. It put their own homestead at risk. "It'll take every cent we can scrape up for the next two years to pay that. He won't pay it."

Henry was crestfallen, seeing that she was right. In fact, the debt dragged on for five years, putting a terrible burden on the Ise family. Henry suffered several bouts of discouragement about this debt and other setbacks, and in his despair he might well have abandoned their claim. But Rosie wouldn't let him. She was the strong one, and she insisted they tough it out. In every functional way, Rosie was as much a homesteader as Henry was.

Olive Bern and her husband Charles, when they homesteaded in Hettinger County, North Dakota, in 1907, depended on each other to make their venture a success. Like most homesteaders, during the early years they needed to purchase as little as possible and earn as much cash from off-farm jobs as they could. They brought clothes from Wisconsin that turned out to be completely unsuited for the prairie, so Olive got busy making clothes for the whole family. She soon outfitted her two sons with overalls and her daughter with Mother Hubbard aprons. She made sunbonnets for everyone.

Olive was a talented seamstress, and she took in custom sewing jobs to supplement the family income. These chores came in addition to cooking, cleaning, preserving, gardening, feeding the chickens, and all the other tasks that fell to her. Without her contributions, the family would have been far less successful.

The Homestead Act and the GLO reflected the customs of the day by defining the husband as "the" homesteader. He was the "head" of the household and filed the claim at the land office. The wife, children, and other household dependents might be mentioned someplace in the GLO paperwork, but otherwise the official transaction was men's business. When the patent came, the husband owned the land.

But if we withdraw from this nineteenth-century mindset and focus instead on how the typical homestead actually worked, we see a rather different arrangement. Homesteading families were much more likely to be successful when the wife and husband formed a mutually supportive and complementary team.

The laws and gender rules of the era allowed the man to dominate, even to be a tyrant, within his family. Swiss-born homesteader Jules Sandoz, who homesteaded in Sheridan County, Nebraska, was cruel and domineering to his four wives, whom he beat viciously. He deserted his first wife, and the second and third escaped him. But he never suffered any legal consequences for his cruelty.

Thomas Raaen, the Norwegian homesteader who settled in Steele County, Dakota Territory, was a violent drunk. When inebriated, he regularly brutalized his wife Ragnhild and terrorized his children. Abraham Calof, a much older North Dakota homesteader, married Rachel Calof, an eighteen-year-old Jewish girl who had traveled from Odessa, Russia, to enter an arranged marriage with him. She found herself trapped in a highly constrained life, limited and mentally dominated by her husband and by the strict gender expectations of her culture. Other examples of domestic abuse among homesteaders are not hard to find.

But homesteading also attracted or developed many strong women. Rosie Ise, Josephine Denio, Jenny Fletcher, Mary Pearl, Ella Oxford, Elizabeth Eubank, Hettie Anderson, Olive Bern, and the other women whose stories are told in prior chapters demonstrated their own strength. In most cases we cannot know the nature of their private marital relations, whether they were harmonious or abusive, but they appear to have formed mutually beneficial partnerships with their husbands.

My own grandmothers showed the possibilities. Rosabell Edwards, a physically imposing woman with a demanding personality, homesteaded in North Dakota in 1902 with her husband Webster. She dominated her morose mate, and when she had had enough, she left him and moved to town with their kids.

Frankie and William Burlingame homesteaded in North Dakota in 1903. Frankie was a small, birdlike figure with an indomitable will; William was a soft spoken and gentle type. They had a decades-long, devoted partnership, lasting until William died. Their daily activities were strictly gender defined: she tended her garden but never worked in the fields; he plowed but never cooked. They lived their long lives as agreeable, loving complements to each other.

Wives and husbands depended on each other, each contributing to the homestead goods or services that the other could not. The author Mari Sandoz, as usual an insightful observer, remarked that "nothing happened [on the farm] after [the wife] arrived that did not vitally touch her." Among her many critical chores, Sandoz noted that "particularly important was her place in accident or sickness, with doctors so few and far between." Also, "when drouth and hail and wind came, it was the housewife who set as good a table as possible from what remained and sustained the morale of her family."

Successful homesteaders typically also relied heavily on helpful nearby neighbors, who provided assistance. Often, women were the ones who maintained these networks, thereby sustaining the life and viability of the family's whole homesteading enterprise.

One task fell entirely to women, and it was an exceptionally dangerous one: childbirth. Virtually all homesteading women who gave birth did so in their own homes. Most were attended by female relatives or women acting as midwives, usually with no formal training and little medical knowledge. Not until the 1910s were rural mothers attended by trained physicians, and even then many were not. The mother's pain was unrelieved by the kinds of interventions that would later become available, such as nitrous oxide, epidurals, and anesthesia.

M. G. Flath trained in obstetrics at Northwestern University Medical College in Chicago. He took a specialization in obstetrics. He arrived to take up a medical practice in the small town of Stanley, North Dakota, in 1911. His long career saw him assist in over three thousand births. He was renowned for fearlessly driving across the prairie, night or day, even during the severest blizzards, to answer the call to assist birthing women on remote farms.

The first birth Flath attended shocked him. He arrived at a farmhouse south of the nearby town of Ross. A midwife, drunk, greeted him with the news that she had examined the mother and, in the midwife's opinion, the mother couldn't have the baby. The doctor, she said, should take (abort) it. Flath feared infection, given the midwife's extremely dirty hands. But he assisted the mother, and after ten hours of labor the mother delivered a healthy baby.

In another case, this time on a farm south of Stanley, Flath was met by a midwife.

She informed him, "This woman cannot have her baby, you'll have to take it. I've done everything I can for her."

"What have you done?"

"Well, I greased her from her waist to her knees, and it hasn't helped a bit."

After cleaning the mother up, Flath was able to help her deliver safely. But many pregnant women on homesteads did not have access to medical help, relying instead on untrained relatives or midwives. Some midwives were careful and effective, but others were not.

Given the poorer sanitary conditions, lack of medical care, and ignorance about sepsis, maternal mortality among homesteading women was likely very high. We lack accurate national statistics on how many women died of childbirth complications in the nineteenth century, but scholars have guessed that the U.S. maternal death rate was between 0.5 and 1 percent of births. This rate implies that out of every one hundred to two hundred births, a woman died. (The current U.S. rate, still very high compared to other western countries, is about one maternal death per three thousand births.)

Since, on average, a married woman gave birth five or more times during her life, her chances of dying from childbirth were at least 2.5–5 percent. But these figures could well represent a vast undercount. And surely childbirth-related deaths in the homesteading areas would likely have been much higher than in the nation at large. All homesteaders, particularly the women, must have known of other women who died giving birth.

Nancy Lenore Benson married Omer Madison Kem in 1874, and they homesteaded about four miles northwest of Broken Bow in Custer County, Nebraska. In 1883 Nancy died, and her death went almost completely unrecorded. Nancy likely died from pregnancy-related complications, as she was described as "leaving three small children, Maude, Laura, and Claude." Omer was considered a highly eligible widower and married again. He wound up with five daughters and three sons from his two marriages.

In 1873 Henry Burden married Eliza Hill. He was then about thirty years old, and as far as we know, he had been alone ever since he fled slavery and certainly since he filed his claim in Nebraska. Eliza undoubtedly brought welcome companionship and much-needed help with the chores on the isolated Saline County homestead. Unfortunately, in 1876, after three years of marriage, she died in childbirth. Henry then married Mary Barbour in 1878. They had a lengthy and compatible marriage. Mary gave birth to eight children in sixteen years: in 1879, 1881,

1883, 1885, 1887, 1889, 1891, and 1893. She died in 1895, likely from complications of childbirth. She joined so many other women for whom pregnancy was a death sentence.

Women also participated in homesteading in a much more dramatic and public way—by claiming land in their own names.

The men in Congress (there were no women) who passed the Homestead Act conventionally expected white families, headed by a man, with his wife, children, and other relatives as dependents, to do the homesteading. However, they did provide for other people to homestead as well. They refused to include a racial exclusion clause, opening the way for Black homesteaders. And they explicitly provided for some women— single (never-married) women and widows—to file claims in their own names; they excluded married women on the grounds that each family should only get one homestead which would be claimed by the husband.

The GLO, charged with implementing the act, subsequently opened homesteading to women who were divorced or could prove they had been abandoned by their husbands, a frequent form of informal divorce among poorer couples. The GLO considered these women as "heads of households," too, the key status that made them eligible to file a claim. Women in all these different situations homesteaded.

In the nineteenth century women filing claims in their own name were relatively rare. Conditions were more primitive, and homesteading regions more isolated, which may have inhibited women filers. More commonly, perhaps, women filed claims to expand their father's or brother's land.

Emma, Ruth, Lizzie, and Lutie Chrisman were daughters of Charles Chrisman, a Custer County, Nebraska, rancher. The four women all filed multiple homestead, timber-culture, and cash-entry claims. The four sisters were famously photographed by Solomon Butcher in 1886, standing in front of what purported to be the sod house in which they were living to fulfill their residency requirement. The grass around the house is suspiciously not worn down, however, suggesting it may have been used more for photo opportunities than as the women's actual residence.

By the turn of the century, solo women became increasingly aware of the opportunities homesteading offered them. Women put their names in for the Rosebud lotteries, some winning claims. After the 1905 drawing, most women with winning tickets chose not to file claims, but 231 single women located themselves on farms. When newspapers reported their success, the women started receiving letters proposing marriage from men who would become farmers if they could obtain a wife and farm. A Wagner, South Dakota, newspaper predicted, "Many will be the romances that will follow the luck of these women in the big land lottery last summer."

Elizabeth Corey was pushed out of the nest at seventeen by her stressed parents. She apparently had little interest in, or maybe little opportunity for, marriage, and she was not overly enthralled with her prospects as a spinster teacher in Iowa. Corey saw homesteading as her way out. She moved to Stanley County, South Dakota, and filed a homestead claim.

Corey was no farmer or builder. She was a teacher, and in a pattern followed by many solo women homesteaders, she used her teaching wages to hire out the heavy farmwork. She hired several men at different times to break her prairie and make fields. Grant Stone built her shack, and Stone and Bess's brother Robert dug her cistern. She lived on her claim for thirty-seven years, only leaving when her health failed.

Isabel Proctor homesteaded in Montana in 1912. She was born in 1884 on a 120-acre farm near Bailey, Iowa. In 1906, at a time when few girls went to college, she entered Iowa State Normal

**Fig. 21.** Six women homesteaders, Haakon County, South Dakota, circa 1915. Permission of South Dakota State Historical Society.

School (later to be called Iowa State Teachers College and now called University of Northern Iowa). At college she played center on the Shakes (the girls basketball team), participated in campus theatrical productions, including "Hamlet," and sang and played piano in concerts with her brother Warren. She graduated with a bachelor's degree in music and German in 1910.

For two years Proctor taught music and English in Iowa and Minnesota schools. Then her brother Mert, a railroad engineer who had settled in eastern Montana, wrote her, saying, "Come out and homestead. The government is giving land away." Like others, she developed Montana Fever. She recruited her college friend Helen Craft to join her, and they filed abutting claims near Rapelje, a remote community in the flatlands of Stillwater County on the western edge of the Great Plains. Mert built a shack for them right on the claim's boundary, half on Isabel's claim and half on Helen's claim, permitting them to live together and still fulfill the residency requirement.

Isabel needed to earn a living, and she found a teaching job in the Rapelje school. Every school day, including those when the bitterest winter winds blew and the snow studded the trail with high drifts, she rode her horse the fifteen miles to Rapelje and back. In 1915, after three years, she and Helen proved up on their homesteads.

Isabel was then free to move on, and she accepted a position at the Stanley (North Dakota) High School. She taught music, geometry, girls' physical education, and German, the latter until the school dropped it during World War I. She married the town dentist, and as Isabel Flath, she would be the town's major musical impresario for the next seven decades.

Lily Bell Stearns homesteaded northwest of Glasgow, in Valley County, Montana, in 1912 with her four children. She had recently divorced their father. She hoped that a piece of the government's free land might give her some stability as she tried to reconstruct her life. But she suffered many setbacks, including a cyclone that destroyed her shack, smashed her dishes, and scattered all her groceries.

But Stearns's biggest problem was her suspicious and hostile neighbors, who according to historian Sara Gregg, plagued her. They disliked her Reformed Latter Day Saints faith. They accused her of sexual license, claiming that she had conducted an affair with her son's employer. And they charged her with dishonesty in her land claim. Maybe their chief motivation, aside from misogyny, was that they wanted her land. Lily Stearns, at a time in her life when a community of helpful neighbors could have made a huge and positive difference, was instead battered by her neighbors' legal and extralegal efforts to force her to relinquish her land.

After they proved up, women had choices to make. They could remain on their farms working the land, they could lease their ground, or they could sell their claims. The first option directly empowered the woman homesteader, but the second and third options did too: homesteading was one of the few avenues by which women could accumulate wealth.

Many homesteading women expected their stays on the land to be temporary. They arrived planning to remain only long enough to prove up and then sell out. They would return home with their booty, perhaps to buy a home, start a business, or go to college. Yet their experiences on the land often changed them and their plans. Colorado homesteader Alice Newberry wrote to her family in 1903 explaining how her homesteading venture that had begun with dreams of a financial windfall ultimately became the source of as much emotional gratification as economic benefit. Elizabeth Corey had no firm plan that her move to South Dakota would be permanent, but she only left her land when she was old and needed cancer treatments.

Isabel Proctor and Nannie Francis chose the second path. Proctor resided on her claim to fulfill her residency requirement but moved away soon after proving up. She retained her land for decades and leased it out to neighboring ranchers. Francis, a California woman, proved up on her Montana claim in 1914 and moved back to California.

Others chose the third option, selling their claims. Lucy Wells of Dawes County, Nebraska, was twenty-one at the time of her final proof. Her husband had died the previous year, so after she received her patent, she sold the homestead and moved back to Iowa. Ellen Abbott, age fifty and also in Dawes County, lost her husband and, the next year, proved up her (their) claim. Abbott sold her farm worth $890 the year she received her patent. She bemoaned the work involved in keeping up such a large farm and wanted to sell it before it lost value from disrepair.

So women filing homestead claims were as varied in their circumstances as the men who filed claims: some were poor, seeking a step up in life, while others who were more favorably situated were attracted by the adventure and the chance to step beyond the bounds of the conventional expectations of women's behavior.

Nannie Francis was one of the poor ones. She was a single mother living in California with two small children, ages three and one. Her husband either was dead or had abandoned her (the stories differ). In 1910 at age thirty-two, Nannie faced poverty and few good prospects. Her uncle Frank West and cousin Lulu West planned to homestead in Montana. They stopped by her house to say goodbye. Nannie made a quick decision—she and the children would join them.

Soon they were on a ship up the coast to Seattle and then riding a Great Northern train to Chouteau County, Montana. They descended at the small settlement of Stanford. They traveled north by wagon to the even smaller crossroads of Dover. They continued on in an overloaded and crowded wagon that bumped over fifty jarring miles of prairie. Finally reaching their destination, Nannie and the others staked out 320-acre claims, which they filed at the land office in Lewistown.

Nannie's claim was raw prairie—no dwelling, no barn, no broken prairie for fields, no farm equipment, no fencing. She knew she could not build all the infrastructure herself. Unfortunately she (and Lulu) lacked money to hire men to build for them. Moreover, her uncle Frank got sick, became discouraged, and left Montana for good. But as Nannie later wrote, "We women didn't give up so easily." They planned to work in town and save their wages to invest in their claims.

They returned to Stanford to search for employment, but no one was hiring. So Nannie and Lulu started a bakery, and they found a growing clientele among the stores and surrounding farm families. Then a couple of cousins persuaded the women to join them in a venture running a hotel in Dover, so they gave up the bakery, sold their baking supplies at a loss, and moved to Dover. Nannie got typhoid and lay in bed for three weeks, and the customers at the hotel in Dover turned out to be mostly drunk and unruly cowhands. Nannie lamented, "We found out the hotel business was not our calling as we came out $200 behind."

For the next couple of years Nannie worked as a cook at the Kennedy ranch, which was owned by two bachelor brothers. She hired men to construct a shack on her homestead. The Kennedys allowed her to return to her claim periodically, staying for a couple of weeks each time to establish the veneer for, as she put it, "satisfying Uncle Sam." She finally proved up her claim in 1914.

But while poor women like Lily Bell Stearns and Nannie Francis constituted the vast majority of women filing claims, more fortunately situated women like Isabel Proctor gained all the acclaim. Indeed, educated pioneering women became a national sensation. During these years urban women were bobbing their hair and wearing shorter skirts as they struggled to break free of Victorian gender constraints and create more life choices for themselves. Jane Addams, Margaret Sanger, and Mary McLeod Bethune became household names. The women's suffrage campaign reached its successful climax during the decade. And single women homesteaders demonstrated a different way in which women could do unexpected things.

The *Atlantic Monthly* and other national publications trumpeted these plucky women, protofeminists, as adventurers. They went into the wilds and established their claims, so the image went, while writing poetry and leading cultured lives.

Mattie T. Cramer, a Montana homesteader, published a letter in the Great Northern Railway *Bulletin* in 1913. It was titled "Success of a 'Lone' Woman." She described Montana as a land of unlimited opportunities, and to prove it, she told her own story. In 1908 she had less than one hundred dollars to her name when she filed a homestead claim in Phillips County. Five years later, she owned a two-story house worth $1,000, a barn and outbuildings, and twenty-one acres planted to crops, plus two lots and a rental house in the town of Malta.

Her letter, which had been solicited by a Great Northern agent, generated a huge response. Other publications reprinted it. Hundreds of women from Missouri, New York, Illinois, and all over the nation wrote to Cramer, requesting more information and sharing their own stories. Nellie Maple from Paris, Illinois, said she was a schoolteacher and wondered, Could she continue teaching while homesteading? And by the way, What are teachers paid in Malta? Harriet Miller wrote to Cramer from Angola, Indiana, saying, "I too am a lone woman have been a widow for nearly 32 years. I too have made some success in life and now have what they call here Montana fever." Miller proved up a homestead in Hill County, Montana, in 1924.

Undoubtedly the one who created the most attention was Elinore Pruitt Stewart with her widely read letters in the *Atlantic Monthly*. The *Atlantic* was a highly influential national publication. It was edited in Boston and read by intellectuals and all the smart set.

Elinore Pruitt had been widowed with a small child and worked as a housekeeper in Denver. In 1909 Henry Clyde Stewart, a widowed Wyoming homesteader, placed an ad in the *Denver Post*. He was looking to hire a housekeeper to help on his homestead near Burntfork, Wyoming. Elinore accepted his offer. She and her three-year-old, Jerrine, arrived at the homestead in March. In early May she filed a claim for a quarter section adjoining Clyde's homestead. A week later she married Clyde, becoming Elinore Pruitt Stewart.

Elinore began writing letters back to her old Denver employer, Juliet Coney, a widow who had retired from her teaching job in Boston before moving to Colorado. Elinore described her l adventures on the Stewart homestead, writing in a forward, earthy style which was sometimes humorous, ......es tragic, and almost always riveting.

On a trip back to Boston, Coney showed Stewart's letters to a friend, Ellery Sedgwick, who was editor of the *Atlantic Monthly*, and she suggested he publish them. Sedgwick was looking for material to publish that had what he termed "a fringe of informality" to leaven the juiceless essays penned by Boston highbrows. He found Elinore's letters charming, and between October 1913 and April 1914, the magazine ran thirteen of Elinore's letters as a continuing series.

The letters were an immediate sensation. She was living proof of the powers of women. (Clyde Stewart faded into the background.) In Sedgwick's words, she was the "woman Homesteader who in the face of every conceivable obstacle had taken up a quarter section in a remote corner of Wyoming. . . . It really mattered very little what life Elinore . . . had been born into. She could have made a go at anything." The *New York Evening Post* declared Elinore's letters to be "the literary discovery of the year." Houghton, Mifflin, a top-drawer Boston publishing house, collected the letters and published them in 1914 as *Letters of a Woman Homesteader*. The *New York Times* reviewed her book. It became a classic and is still in print.

Elinore perfectly embodied the grit, determination, honesty, plainspoken bluntness, and inherent uprightness that avant-garde eastern readers prized in their western heroes. She confirmed their preconceptions of the hardy qualities that won the West. That she could overcome the challenges of a Wyoming homestead and describe her experiences in such engaging, authentic prose only served as confirmation of women's powers.

It was only many years later that the rest of Elinore's story came out. Because Elinore had filed her homestead claim as a single woman and wed Clyde the next week, she worried about the legality of her claim. So she relinquished her claim to her mother-in-law, Ruth Stewart. When Ruth later received her patent, she promptly sold the claim to Clyde for a hundred dollars. Although never detected by the GLO or its agents, Elinore's transactions arguably violated the marital rules of homesteading and constituted land fraud.

Many other solo female homesteaders added to the public stir when they wrote about their own experiences and found editors eager to publish their accounts. Elizabeth Abbey Everett wrote a piece for *The Independent* in 1913 that began, "The day I was twenty-one my Uncle Sam offered me a farm for a birthday present."

Metta Loomis published "From Schoolroom to Montana Ranch" in the *Overland Monthly* in 1916. She wrote, "The lone woman is almost incapacitated for homesteading, and her first move towards entering a claim for a homestead should be to induce some other woman to join her. Two women taking up adjoining claims can [do the job]." Mildred Hunt and her friend Sophie Maud Jefferson homesteaded adjacent properties in Chouteau County, Montana, and built their shacks, each on their own claims, side by side.

That same year Cecelia Weiss published "Homesteading Without a Chaperon" in *Sunset* magazine. Unmarried, she filed on land adjoining her married sister's claim and recounted her struggles to make her farm pay. "My 320 acres do not support me—yet I support them." "Disregarding whatever pecuniary gain there may be," she wrote, "it is a real inspiration to be part of a modern pioneer colony conquering the wilderness."

"Why do divorcees prefer to take a chance in a new country rather than a flyer in the matrimonial market again?" Mary Isabel Brush asked this question in 1911 in the pages of *Colliers*, the wildly popular mass-market national magazine. Her answer was the same as the ones she gave for why a soft-voiced, tenderly

**Fig. 22.** Dwellings of Mildred Hunt and Sophie Maud Jefferson (homesteaders in Chouteau County, Montana, 1914), who built their shacks near each other, each on her own claim. Permission of Overholser Historical Research Center.

raised woman would deliberately relinquish a life of comfort, why stenographers would give up private secretaryships, and why young girls from good families ("where nothing more is required of them than to wash a few dishes") would travel to "civilization's end" to claim a homestead. Her answer was given in the article's title: "Woman on the Prairies: Pioneers Who Win Independence and Freedom in Their One-Room Homes."

So solo women homesteaders became a national fascination. Magazines made claiming land appear as a kind of adventuresome lark, the claimant living near nature, building her financial reserves, establishing her independence, and maybe using her free time to write lyric poetry or read Shakespeare. These publications portrayed homesteading as a way for young single women from good families (and some older women too), to accrue a bit of capital, a feat almost impossible to achieve on the wages of poorly paid teachers, nurses, telephone operators, or housekeepers. It was an alternative to marrying well, an option some young women may not have had available or desired.

Solo women homesteaders used the Homestead Act differently from solo men or couples. While we certainly have examples of solo women building their shacks, plowing and fencing their fields, and doing all the other heavy work that men did, these cases are rare. Instead, most single women hired such work to be done. They filed their claims and then worked in restaurants and banks or as teachers, nurses, midwives, or cooks. They saved their earnings to hire men to build their dwellings, construct barns, put up fencing, break the prairie, and plant and harvest crops.

Women's homesteading followed a different pattern from the traditional settler approach in which the farm family did most of the jobs on the farm themselves. Solo women home- steaders simply developed a new way to make the Homestead Act work for them.

This step forward for women was met, as such steps often are, by resistance from men. Men, especially other homesteaders sim- ilar to those who lusted after Lily Bell Stearns's land, complained that women homesteaders weren't "real" homesteaders—that it was unfair that they could claim land when they didn't actually farm it themselves.

Official Washington agreed. The Roosevelt Administration had received worrying reports that lumber companies were abusing the Homestead Act in northern Michigan and Minnesota. The companies would pay front men to file claims; these men would strip the land of its standing timber. They would then abandon the ruined tracts, never intending to be "actual settlers." So in 1904 President Roosevelt created a Public Land Commission, headed by Gifford Pinchot, to investigate fraud in the program. Before it began collecting evidence, the commission took care to equip itself with its conclusion—fraud was rampant.

But the commission reported one surprising finding seemingly beyond its remit: women were homesteading too. Members were shocked that "a large percentage of commuted [purchased] entries are made by females." Moreover, they said, "Investigation has shown that the residence of females consists of mere visits to their homestead entries once or twice every six months, and their improvements, if any, have been made by others, generally relatives, and are simply sufficient to pass their proofs; that as soon as commutation has been accomplished they cease to make even visits or cultivate the entries, and sell same as quickly as a purchaser can be found." Finally, almost in exasperation, they concluded, "They are single, and will swear that they have no other home than their entries and were compelled to work out to support themselves."

Digging deeper, the commissioners found an even more shocking practice: "Many entries are made by female schoolteachers, who spend their vacations on their claims, commute their entries, and leave the country as soon as a better paying position can be found elsewhere." The commission intimated that such use of the homestead law by schoolteachers and other solo women perverted its intent and in effect amounted to fraud.

Perhaps Pinchot and his co-commissioners did not have the opportunity to interview homesteaders like Isabel Proctor, who maintained her ownership for decades, or Nannie Francis, who desperately moved from bakery to hotel to housekeeping trying to feed her family while developing her claim. Unfortunately for the commission, neither the Homestead Act nor GLO regulations required that the homesteader construct her dwelling herself or plow her required ten acres herself. Strangely, neither the commissioners nor anyone else charged fraud when men, "real" heads of households, hired others to build their houses or break their prairie sod.

Married men filed about 66 percent of all successful homestead claims—that is, married couples claimed 66 percent of homesteads for which the husband filed the papers. Single men filed on about 18 percent of claims, and single women on perhaps 11 percent. Of the filings by single men, 5 percent were by men who were widowed, separated, divorced, or for whom no information is available. So men participated in 89 percent of all homesteads, and women in 77 percent. Homesteaders were nearly as likely to be women as men.

How many solo women homesteaders were there? Plausible estimates suggest that as many as 292,000 solo women filed initial claims, and somewhere around 160,000 succeeded in obtaining their patents. Their success rate, 55 percent, was nearly identical to the rate for all homesteaders.

National magazines romanticized solo women's homesteading experiences. But there were many more cases like Corey, Francis, and Stearns, women who struggled and suffered setbacks before succeeding, than there were easier cases like Cramer and Proctor. It was women's grit and determination that led to most successful claims. And when such women wrote about their experiences, they confessed to loneliness, anxiety, depression, fear, and incessant worry, as well as pride in their accomplishments.

Katherine Harris studied solo women homesteaders in Colorado's South Platte valley. She found that the Homestead Act did in fact open important new opportunities for women. Harris noted that "homesteading, like life, dealt a complex and sometimes subtle mix of successes and failures." She found that women's increased agency and opportunity were directly linked to the power they derived from owning land. Their power as landowners altered the balance in gender relations.

When women enjoyed some of the same economic choices as men, especially in the context of the labor shortages that were ubiquitous in homesteading areas, they felt freer to venture outside conventional gender roles. Homesteading encouraged women to enlarge the scope of their activities in their communities, and it brought them greater power and responsibility within their families. Simply put, as Harris noted, women exercised more power because they owned land.

# CHAPTER TEN

# The Homesteaders' Legacy

Homesteading was largely over by the late 1920s. What was its legacy?

Homesteading ended after the disastrous 1921 collapse in crop prices. Farmers struggled throughout the rest of the decade to overcome low prices and drought-driven declining harvests. They entered the 1930s already weakened, and they were then hit with the true calamity of the Great Depression. This unrewarding and unpromising situation for farmers discouraged people from becoming homesteaders. President Franklin Roosevelt signed a series of laws and issued two executive orders in 1934 and 1935 that effectively ended homesteading by withdrawing the bulk of federal land (except in Alaska) from the "unreserved and unappropriated public domain"—that is, land that was open for homesteading.

Only the large food demands of World War II and the consumerist society that emerged after it brought prosperity back to farmers. By then American agriculture had been transformed again, with fewer farmers working much bigger and more mechanized farms. Many homesteaders had left. In 1920 Great Plains farmers numbered 747, 262. Over the next three decades, one out of five of them, 152,826 in all, left farming.

Some have pointed to the large number of initial filers who failed to earn patents, about 45 percent, as evidence that homesteading failed. Others argue that the law's failure can be seen in the many successful filers who later left their land. Some scholars even suggest that the continuing depopulation of the region's rural areas is a mark of homesteading's failure because the program encouraged too many people to move to farms.

More reasonably, homesteaders were like all nineteenth- and twentieth-century American farmers—they were subjected to two long-term trends that reduced rural populations. One was that the changes in agricultural technology favored larger farms. John Deere and others rolled out bigger plows and harrows, more powerful tractors, and gigantic harvesters. The ever-larger machinery made it possible for fewer farmers to farm more land.

The second trend was that national and international food markets incessantly drove food-crop prices down (except during unusual periods like 1915 to 1921). Farmers tried to make up for receiving lower prices by growing more grain to sell. Both trends pushed farmers to expand the size of their farms. Some farmers succeeded in getting bigger; others sold out, reducing the number of farmers.

But in its heyday (the half-century from 1870 to 1920), homesteading was a powerful force. Congress passed the Homestead Act in the midst of civil war as the definitive antidote to the Slave Power's dream of territorial expansion. That antidote turned out to be unnecessary because war and the Thirteenth Amendment settled the slavery issue.

Congress intended the Homestead Act to provide the model for settlement of the interior West by "actual settlers" rather than speculators, cattle barons, and bonanza farmers. In this it was largely successful: in the regions favorable to farming, homesteaders created a dense society of family farmers that has mostly persisted down to the present day, even as individual farms grew bigger. Only in the drier regions, where row crops withered four years out of five and the land favored grazing, did ranchers agglomerate much larger spreads than the Homestead Act allowed. Many family farms today trace their origins to their ancestors' homesteads.

Homesteading's most visible legacy was the physical transformation of the land. Homesteaders broke immense swathes of Great Plains prairie to establish their farms. In doing so, they continued the great plow-up that started in Ohio and swept west. Homesteaders simply carried out the last phase of "breaking" the land.

Few in American society challenged the plow-up, and most cheered. The vast North American grassland, one of the great biomes of the planet and home to enormous biological diversity, was never considered worthy of conserving until it was too late. Conservationists from John Muir to Teddy Roosevelt cherished the mountains of Yellowstone and Yosemite and the splendors of the Grand Canyon and New England's rocky coast. But few saw the grassland as something worth saving. Federal officials located no extensive national parks in the Great Plains—Badlands National Park in South Dakota, not established until 1978, is only the nineteenth largest park in the lower forty-eight states.

As a result, the tallgrass prairie, most of which lies east of the Great Plains but which extends into central Nebraska and Kansas, was almost completely plowed under. Only 1 to 3 percent of it remains, mostly in small islands of miraculously saved patches like the 11,000 acre National Tallgrass Prairie Preserve in Kansas.

The mixed-grass prairie is a two-hundred-mile-wide strip covering the drier central and western parts of the stack of states from Texas to North Dakota. It was also mostly plowed under. Today only about 20 to 30 percent of the mixed-grass prairie remains. Even much of the more arid shortgrass prairie, which runs from the western edge of the mixed-grass prairie to the Rocky Mountain foothills, has been put under the plow. From 40 to 70 percent of it remains. One study found that farmers have plowed about a third of the land area of the Great Plains. And the big plow-up continues. In 2020 landowners converted another 1.8 million acres of prairie into cropland.

By plowing the prairie the homesteaders transformed the Great Plains into a food-producing colossus. Its farmers today produce nearly a quarter of the food grown in the United States, with much higher percentages of wheat, soybeans, and beef.

Homesteaders and their family members added nearly five million people to the population of the Great Plains. Many others were attracted to the region by the lure of free land but ultimately decided to buy land from the railroads or speculators or take up employment in the region's towns and cities. Homesteading was thus the main reason the populations of Kansas, Nebraska, the Dakotas, and other states boomed, just as homesteading's demise after 1920 explains why those states' populations grew very slowly afterward.

The Indigenous nations of the region were disrupted and defeated, disorganizing their societies and dispiriting their people. This was part of a larger story growing out of the United States' exuberant growth during the nineteenth century, including massive growth in population and industrial strength and military power. Growth overrode all obstacles—mountainous terrain and physical distance and civil war—and it overcame Indian opposition as well. The government relocated some tribes to Indian Territory (present-day Oklahoma) and restricted others to shrinking reservation lands.

Homesteaders played little role in this process during homesteading's first phase. But in its second phase, when land seekers moved deeper into the Dakotas and Montana and Oklahoma, some came into greater contact with Indians and intruded on reservation lands. Presidents Harrison and T. R. Roosevelt reduced the size of reservations, implemented the Dawes Act allotments, and opened to homesteading "surplus" lands—that is, tribal reservation land remaining after the government had made individual acreage allotments to Native families.

These intrusions proved particularly damaging to the tribes' efforts to reestablish Indian life and culture within their changed circumstances. They produced, for example, a "checkerboard" pattern of landholdings in which white farmers were interspersed with remaining Indian holdings, making communal Native management of the landscape nearly impossible.

Given the great disparities in population and power, the process ended with Native peoples occupying much less land at the end of the period than at the beginning. The government's program, whether intentionally or not, was careless and uncaring of the Indians' well-being. Some homesteaders assisted dispossession and benefited from it.

The government's experiment in giving away land generated local communities that were deeply committed to democratic customs. The very principle of making grants to ordinary people and limiting them to 160 acres, more in the drier parts of the West, was democratic in itself. At proving-up, the GLO required claimants to rely on their neighbors (excluding close relatives) to provide affidavits certifying residency.

Homesteading created a society of small property holders that was much more egalitarian than our modern urban culture is, with its wide divisions between the rich and poor. It prompted neighbors to work together and make decisions together concerning matters that affected them all. They cooperated to organize and run schools, manage roads, build churches, and deal with common threats like prairie fires.

Homesteading fostered in rural neighborhoods what we may recognize as informal habits of democratic practice. Voting was typically not the most important decision mechanism for local decisions. Rather, neighbors found that consultation and a search for agreement worked better, although they reverted to formal mechanisms when harmony broke down.

This communal and participatory way of interacting with neighbors was surprisingly inclusive in some ways, not so in others. It typically included people of vastly different nationalities, languages, customs, religions, and aspirations. Charles Bern, on his Hettinger County, North Dakota, claim, was Swedish and Lutheran. He and his family learned to cooperate with and depend on neighbors in his own section who were Irish and Catholic, Dutch, and native-born. Beyond section twenty, the Berns found people of other ethnicities, languages, and religions with whom they needed to cooperate. Historian Eric Foner observes about this period that "the most multicultural state in the Union was North Dakota."

Mary Burden, a Black homesteader in Saline County, Nebraska, teamed up with neighboring Czech women. During weekend socializing, her family mingled with the nearby whites, which included putting all the children to bed together as they got tuckered out.

The limits of democratic practice were visible too. It certainly did not include Native Americans at all. Black people were accepted in some places and not others: the Burden family was well integrated into local society in Saline County, and Oscar Micheaux in Gregory County, South Dakota. But others, like the Black settlers at Empire in Goshen County, Wyoming, were ostracized and shut out. Lutherans, Catholics, Mormons, Baptists, Methodists, AME congregants, Presbyterians, and Pentecostals sometimes let their differing devotional affiliations create suspicion and hostility, making it hard for them to collaborate.

Women were restricted to narrower participation in local democratic practices than were men, an aspect of the pervasive gender norms of the day. But there were some surprising exceptions. Rural residents voted to choose their township officers, school boards, church diaconal boards, county commissioners, and other local officials. Women in many Great Plains states voted in these elections long before they were enfranchised in national elections. In Dakota Territory women voted in school elections as early as 1879, and women in Wyoming, Montana, and other states voted in local or state elections well before the Nineteenth Amendment to the U.S. constitution was ratified in 1920. Jennette Rankin, elected to the U.S. Congress from Montana in 1916, was the first woman to serve in that body. Still, it was rare that women took the lead or participated fully in matters of public business.

For rural families, cooperation enforced by necessity did not come without tension; necessary cooperation sometimes even brought violence. Henry and Mary Ise in the 1880s suffered stress and loss of friends when the nasty road dispute broke out in their Osborne County, Kansas, neighborhood. Each side hired lawyers and engaged in a years-long battle. It left bad feelings and lingering grudges all around.

In Mountrail County, North Dakota, Verne Hagey, a rambunctious young man, grew up on his parents' homestead. He and his native-born "American" friends often provoked fistfights with young men in the nearby Finnish settlement of Belden. They especially liked to pick up girls at Belden's Saturday night dances, infuriating the young Finnish men.

In 1922 Anna Niemi, Finnish and just sixteen years old, and Tom Scrivener, native-born and a few years older, fell in love. Anna got pregnant, and they married. The couple seemed happy, especially after the birth of their daughter. But Finnish toughs hated Tom Scrivener for taking away one of "their" girls. It appears (nothing was proved definitively) that they accosted him one evening as he was driving his wagon home from town. They threw him down a deep abandoned well. Searchers discovered his broken, lifeless body the next day.

Such disputes were usually resolved by older, more responsible community leaders and through appeal to justices of the peace, local pastors, coroners, and the like. In the Scrivener case, the local state's attorney lacked clear evidence and filed no charges.

The democratic practices of rural neighborhoods shaped the culture of Great Plains towns as well. When homesteaders moved to town, they brought with them norms and habits and expectations of rights they had developed and exercised in the countryside. The result was that small towns in the Great Plains tended to be democratic places of extensive community involvement.

As dramatically as homesteading reshaped the land, it transformed the homesteaders even more. Not all families that successfully earned homestead patents remained in farming. Some claimants and their descendants continued in farming, while others took up other professions. Regardless, future generations were shaped by the experiences of their homesteading ancestors. The Homestead Act provided the first rung on the ladder of upward mobility.

Among those who failed to win their patents, some found they had simply wasted their time and toil. Yet even unsuccessful filers may have gained from their experience. They may have acquired skills that they used successfully in their next venture, and some profited by selling their claims as relinquishments.

Among the 960,000 Great Plains families who successfully proved up, the benefits were clearer. Most of the homestead filers were poor. That is the essential truth behind historian Kari Leigh Merritt's observation that, "to this day, the Homestead

Act remains the most comprehensive form of wealth redistribution that has ever taken place in America." Homesteaders who obtained patents gained ownership of a valuable asset, undoubtedly improving their economic standing. Whether the asset gained was worth the toil and sacrifice required to obtain it only the homesteaders themselves could say.

We have some idea of the homesteaders' influence down the generations due to a clever study by the demographer Trina Shanks, now at the University of Michigan. Using marriage rates, female fertility, and other data, Shanks calculated how many people alive at the time of her study (2005) had at least one ancestor who had been a homesteader. Her startling conclusion: *forty-six million*. And if she slightly varied her beginning assumptions, still keeping them in the plausible range, her estimate of living descendants ballooned to ninety-two million, or nearly a third of the U.S. population. In a separate calculation, following Shanks' method, I estimated that roughly 250,000 people alive today are descendants of Black homesteaders.

The homesteaders were shaped in subtle and profound ways by their experiences. Homesteading fostered a distinctive way of thinking about and behaving in the world. Human nature is constant across differences in region and economic circumstance. But how human behavior and beliefs are shaped by people's environments—that is, which attributes, propensities, and values are encouraged and which are suppressed—is not constant.

Homesteading tended to promote a constellation of attributes, values, and habits of mind that became characteristic of the region and the time. It fostered a belief in how an upstanding person ought to behave in the world. It encouraged character traits—call them virtues, for lack of a better word—that people of the region admired in others and strived to achieve in themselves.

Many homesteaders were religious, and they found themselves in circumstances where they felt exceptionally vulnerable to uncontrollable forces. They saw weather, illness, accidents, prairie fires, and locusts as acts of God. They prayed for divine protection, and their vulnerability strengthened their faith. As a result, many expressed their ideas about how to live the good life in religious terms, but their daily experiences facing the challenges of homesteading shaped their beliefs and how they understood their faiths.

Homesteading encouraged individuals to be resolute—to develop a kind of implacable acceptance or embrace of what needed to be done and then to go ahead and do it. It fostered steadfastness, which was seen as being the kind of person others could count on over the long haul. It valued pluck, the willingness to be bold in grabbing opportunity when it came along. It demanded keeping one's word and being honest, the kind of reflexive honesty which required no calculation or assessment of advantages.

Homesteaders admired insistent, dauntless optimism. They believed it was good to find the positives in any situation and act on them, and they believed that being positive was a personal choice. Their attitude contrasted with our modern viewpoint, which finds us more likely to call a therapist.

They appreciated a spirit of adventure—most had extremely limited means and possessions, but they nonetheless delighted in finding ways to create amusement for themselves. They depended on their neighbors and encouraged devotion to community. They revered people who pitched in to help others without expecting anything in return. And they believed in—they almost demanded—personal modesty and they maintained a strong dislike of self-promotion, showing off, or anyone "putting on airs."

This constellation of virtues is how they wanted to be. They are attributes that people implicitly understood to be right, a kind of internal guide or conscience such that when they acted this way they felt good about themselves and when they failed to do so they knew they had fallen short. They admired others who displayed these virtues and thought less of those who did not.

Alas, homesteaders were human, no better at being virtuous or shunning venal behavior than others. They were as subject to the same sins of greed, envy, lust, anger, and pride that tempted other people. Not all homesteaders tried to model their lives on the admired virtues, and of those who did, not all succeeded or succeeded all the time.

Still, the constellation of values and admired virtues that a place or an era raises up is not unimportant. A society usually gets what it celebrates. So if, as at present in our national society, it celebrates wealth and celebrity and being a winner (and belittling losers), people will scramble to achieve those attributes. The homesteading generation celebrated a different set of personal virtues, ones centered on personal responsibility, honesty, and modesty. And their impact was not limited to their own generation—they shaped the lives of their many descendants as well. This is the legacy the homesteaders bequeathed us.

## ACKNOWLEDGMENTS

I want to thank the following friends who read the manuscript and gave me helpful suggestions: Robert Anderson, Margery Davies, George Edwards, Jack Edwards, Mark Engler, Kathleen Hughes, Peter Longo, Arthur MacEwan, Becca Edwards Mayhew, and Laureen Riedesel.

I thank Katie Nieland for her excellent mapmaking and Adam Edwards Mayhew for his wonderful original drawings. Ellen Hurst provided excellent copyediting. Bridget Barry and her colleagues at the University of Nebraska Press believed in this series and this book, which I much appreciate.

# SUGGESTED READING

Alberts, Frances Jacobs. *Sod House Memories*. Vols. 1–3. Hastings NE: Sod House Society, 1972.

Carter, Sarah. *Montana Women Homesteaders: A Field of One's Own*. Helena MT: Far Country Press, 2009.

Cather, Willa, *My Ántonia*. Boston: Houghton Mifflin, 1918.

Edwards, Richard. *Natives of a Dry Place: Stories of Dakota Before the Oil Boom*. Pierre: South Dakota Historical Society Press, 2015.

Edwards, Richard, Jacob Friefeld, and Rebecca Wingo. *Homesteading the Plains: Toward a New History*. Lincoln: University of Nebraska Press, 2017.

Edwards, Richard, and Jacob Friefeld. *The First Migrants: How Black Homesteaders' Quest for Land and Freedom Heralded America's Great Migration*. Lincoln: University of Nebraska Press, 2023.

Gerber, Phillip, ed. *Bachelor Bess: The Homesteading Letters of Elizabeth Corey, 1909–1919*. Iowa City: University of Iowa Press, 1990.

Hansen, Karen V. *Encounter on the Great Plains: Scandinavian Settlers and the Dispossession of Dakota Indians, 1880–1930*. New York: Oxford, 2013.

Ise, John. *Sod and Stubble: The Story of a Kansas Homestead*. Lincoln: University of Nebraska Press, 1936.

Kohl, Edith Eudora. *Land of the Burnt Thigh*. St. Paul: Minnesota Historical Society Press, 1986.

Lockwood, Jefferey. *Locust: The Devastating Rise and Mysterious Disappearance of the Insect That Shaped the American Frontier*. New York: Basic Books, 2004.

Rölvaag, O.E. *Giants in the Earth: A Saga of the Prairie*. New York: Harper & Row, 1927.

Sandoz, Mari. *Old Jules*. Boston: Little, Brown, 1935.

# INDEX

IN THE DISCOVER THE GREAT PLAINS SERIES

*Great Plains Forts*
Jay H. Buckley
and Jeffery D. Nokes

*Great Plains Weather*
Kenneth F. Dewey

*Great Plains Geology*
R. F. Diffendal Jr.

*Great Plains
Homesteaders*
Richard Edwards

*Great Plains Politics*
Peter J. Longo

*Great Plains Bison*
Dan O'Brien

*Great Plains Birds*
Larkin Powell

*Great Plains Literature*
Linda Ray Pratt

*Great Plains Indians*
David J. Wishart

Discover the Great Plains, a series from the Center for Great
Plains Studies and the University of Nebraska Press, offers concise
introductions to the natural wonders, diverse cultures, history,
and contemporary life of the Great Plains. To order or obtain
more information on these or other University of Nebraska Press
titles, visit nebraskapress.unl.edu.